Many churches and leaders today want the popularity of *it* but fail to understand the principles it takes. Because I have seen *it* happen in my own ministry, I know that popularity will fade but principles will last, and I'm telling you that if you apply Craig's seven fundamental ingredients, *it* will take your ministry from good to great. This book is an essential tool for every church leader. Craig is real and authentic and teaches from a place of experience that we all need.

—MICHAEL TODD, #1 *New York Times* bestselling
author; lead pastor, Transformation Church

Some organizations have the *it* factor. Some don't. You may wonder, "Do I have *it*?" If you want the answer, you can find it here. Your leadership has never mattered more than it does right now. Read this book so you can lead like *it* matters.

—JOHN C. MAXWELL, Maxwell Leadership

Wow. Every pastor, every minister, every church employee and volunteer *has* to read this amazing book and give a copy to his or her colleagues. And then they must talk about *it*. Groeschel has identified something that is essential, transformational, and ridiculously important.

—PATRICK LENCIONI, consultant, *New York Times*
bestselling author, and follower of Jesus

With so much discussion around the *it* factor, who doesn't want *it*? Not only does Pastor Craig help identify what *it* is, he aptly teaches us how to find it. This is more than just a book; this is the message of Craig's heart. Not only has he helped me identify the leader in me, I know he will help identify the leader in you. Go for *it!*

—BIANCA JUAREZ OLTHOFF, pastor, The Father's House OC;
podcaster; bestselling author, *How to Have Your Life Not Suck*

When it comes to leadership, my friend Craig Groeschel has *it*. He is one of the best leaders I know in any space. The quality of his work and of his team are the proof that you should read and implement every word in this book. Don't hesitate. Do it!

—DAVE RAMSEY, #1 bestselling author

My friend Craig Groeschel is the visionary and pioneer of America's largest church. In *Lead Like It Matters*, he's generous enough to share the most important lessons he's learned along the way. This isn't just an insightful and interesting book; it's a gamechanging guide to leading with purpose.

—STEVEN FURTICK, lead pastor, Elevation Church; *New York Times* bestselling author, *Crash the Chatterbox*, *Greater*, and *(Un)Qualified*

In *Lead Like It Matters*, Craig wholeheartedly and unreservedly pours out hard-earned wisdom, insight, knowledge, and understanding that are vital to build a thriving church. This book is a gift from one of the greatest church leaders in history. It will inspire, equip, and empower church leaders not only to identify *it* but to learn to sustain and protect it.

—CHRISTINE CAINE, founder, A21 and Propel Women

LEAD
LIKE IT
MATTERS

ALSO BY CRAIG GROESCHEL

LEAD LIKE IT MATTERS

7 Leadership Principles for a Church That Lasts

CRAIG GROESCHEL

ZONDERVAN
BOOKS

ZONDERVAN BOOKS

Lead Like It Matters
Copyright © 2022 by Craig Groeschel

This is a significantly revised and updated edition of *It*, copyright © 2008 by Craig Groeschel.

Requests for information should be addressed to:
Zondervan, *3900 Sparks Dr. SE, Grand Rapids, Michigan 49546*

Zondervan titles may be purchased in bulk for educational, business, fundraising, or sales promotional use. For information, please email SpecialMarkets@Zondervan.com.

ISBN 978-0-310-36283-8 (hardcover)
ISBN 978-0-310-36616-4 (international trade paper edition)
ISBN 978-0-310-36285-2 (audio)
ISBN 978-0-310-36284-5 (ebook)

All Scripture quotations, unless otherwise indicated, are taken from The Holy Bible, New International Version®, NIV®. Copyright © 1973, 1978, 1984, 2011 by Biblica, Inc.® Used by permission of Zondervan. All rights reserved worldwide. www.Zondervan.com. The "NIV" and "New International Version" are trademarks registered in the United States Patent and Trademark Office by Biblica, Inc.®

Scripture quotations marked AMP are taken from the Amplified® Bible. Copyright © 1954, 1958, 1962, 1964, 1965, 1987, 2015 by The Lockman Foundation. Used by permission. (www.Lockman.org).

Scripture quotations marked GW are taken from *God's Word*®. Copyright © 1995 God's Word to the Nations. Used by permission of Baker Publishing Group. All rights reserved.

Scripture quotations marked KJV are taken from the King James Version. Public domain.

Scripture quotations marked MSG are taken from *THE MESSAGE*. Copyright © 1993, 2002, 2018 by Eugene H. Peterson. Used by permission of NavPress. All rights reserved. Represented by Tyndale House Publishers, Inc.

Scripture quotations marked NASB are taken from the (NASB®) New American Standard Bible®, Copyright © 1960, 1971, 1977, 1995, 2020 by The Lockman Foundation. Used by permission. All rights reserved. www.lockman.org

Scripture quotations marked NKJV are taken from the New King James Version®. Copyright © 1982 by Thomas Nelson. Used by permission. All rights reserved.

Scripture quotations marked NLT are taken from the Holy Bible, New Living Translation. © 1996, 2004, 2015 by Tyndale House Foundation. Used by permission of Tyndale House Publishers, Inc., Carol Stream, Illinois 60188. All rights reserved.

The Scripture quotations marked NRSV are taken from the New Revised Standard Version Bible. Copyright © 1989, Division of Christian Education of the National Council of the Churches of Christ in the United States of America. Used by permission. All rights reserved.

Any internet addresses (websites, blogs, etc.) and telephone numbers in this book are offered as a resource. They are not intended in any way to be or imply an endorsement by Zondervan, nor does Zondervan vouch for the content of these sites and numbers for the life of this book.

Craig Groeschel is represented by Thomas J. Winters of Winters & King, Inc., Tulsa, Oklahoma.

Cover design: Stephen Cox
Author photo: Life.Church
Interior design: Denise Froehlich

Printed in the United States of America

22 23 24 25 26 /LSC/ 10 9 8 7 6 5 4 3 2 1

This book is dedicated to my pastor, Nick Harris.

I would not be a pastor without your influence. I am grateful for the impact you have made on me and so many others. You are a hero and spiritual father to me.

The Bible says to give honor to those who deserve honor.

That's you.

I honor you.

I love you.

I miss you.

See you again in heaven.

Thank you for purchasing *Lead Like It Matters*! All of the author's proceeds from this book will be donated to start new churches.

Contents

Preface

In 2008, Britney Spears made a comeback, Brangelina (Pitt and Jolie) welcomed twins, stock markets around the world plunged with the fears of a global recession, and I released a book, *It: How Church Leaders Can Get It and Keep It*. (I'm guessing you don't remember my book release. No offense taken.)

At the time of publishing the book, our church, Life.Church, was twelve years old and I was still in my late thirties. By the grace of God, many pastors and church leaders around the world gravitated toward the concepts in this book. Some said *It* put into words something they knew and felt but never could quite explain. A few pastors said the book helped them keep going and not quit on their churches. Still other ministry leaders said that *It* sparked a fire in them and their churches that burns to this day.

Of all the books I've written, this one is probably my favorite. Why? Because I love the church with all my heart. Not just our church. *The* church. God's church.

Today, Life.Church has been doing ministry for well over a quarter of a century. Our church defied the odds and continued to grow, expand, and thrive well into its third decade. I want to share what we've learned so you can build a church that lasts.

Looking back at the ideas I expressed in 2008, from an earlier season in ministry, I'm shocked at what I think I got right. I was still a young student of leadership and church growth. Yet with the help of a few trusted leaders, we selected seven principles we found were being followed in churches that had *it*. (I'll explain what *it* is and isn't throughout the book.) Even if I started this book from scratch today with much more experience and knowledge, I'd still choose to write about these seven principles.

While I'm amazed at what I think I got right, I'm also shocked at what I didn't know and didn't say. Now, in my midfifties, I've found that my insight, views, and understanding of spiritual leadership have matured more than I anticipated. I knew I had a lot to learn in the years to come. I just had no idea how much! As they say, you don't know what you don't know. That's why I'm revising and expanding this book. I've been told it was helpful in 2008, but the world is different now, and I have so much more to share.

Consider what has changed since 2008. In 2008, the iPhone was brand new and almost no one had one. You thought your flip phone was lit. (Except you *didn't* think that, because back then lit meant drunk, not cool.) In 2008, Instagram and Snapchat did not exist. (Which kind of makes you wonder: Did *you* exist? If you couldn't share your opinions or your photos, how did you live?!) In 2008, if you wanted to go somewhere, you hailed a taxi, because Uber was not yet on the scene. If you were driving and didn't know how to get where you were going, hopefully you owned a GPS, because there wasn't an app for that on your phone. In 2008, Friday nights were for Blockbuster. (Going to a video store and looking for a movie sounds a little prehistoric now.) Of course, if you were super hip, you had a Netflix account, which meant you would order a movie and Netflix would mail a DVD to your house!

So many things are different today than they were in 2008, and to me, the pace of change in the world felt exhilarating. It felt that way until early spring of 2020, when several factors led to what felt like a seismic shift. It started when COVID-19 arrived. Overnight, people were getting sick, some were dying, and suddenly, we faced the explosion of this mysterious virus and the shutdown that followed. All of us were stuck in our homes and developed new ways of living. In the midst of a global pandemic, we were confronted with a powder keg of issues of ongoing racial injustice and tensions, followed by political division and polarization.

So. Much. Change.

Then again, so much has not changed. In 2008, people loved ice cream. They still do. Back then, people liked to belong, to fit in, to matter. They still do. People dreamed of getting married, having a career, raising good kids, making a difference. Today, most still aspire to those things.

So much is different.

So much is the same.

The same is true in churches across the world. Some things are new. Online streaming is a thing, especially after churches couldn't gather physically for months at a time. It didn't used to be. Social media is a part of many churches' strategy. That would have seemed silly not long ago. Worship styles have evolved in many churches. Buildings often look and feel different. How pastors are formally (or not formally) trained has morphed in many parts of the world. What has not changed is the church's mission. We are still called to be the hands and feet of Jesus. We are still charged by Jesus to go into all the world, preach his kingdom, serve people, and make disciples.

As a result of the COVID-19 pandemic, pastors and church leaders are asking different questions. Instead of wanting to know how to launch a contemporary service or move to multisite, many are wondering, *What is the future of the church? Will we ever go back to normal? Can we create a new and better normal?*

In light of all the dramatic changes, while acknowledging what has stayed the same, I felt compelled to update this book.

I'll share with you all kinds of new things I've learned, like:

- What it really means to be people focused and Jesus centered.
- Why we must allow for in-process conversions.
- How we should obsess with giving keys and T-shirts.

It's embarrassing, but I will acknowledge where I got it wrong in the past. One glaring example is with the goal of engagement. Churches need to engage believers with the broader life and activities of the church for spiritual growth and community impact. In the past, I wholeheartedly believed we had to get people in church to engage them during the week. I was wrong. Instead, our goal should be to engage them during the week *where they are*. (That would include their commutes, offices, homes, and digital devices.) To have any chance of their worshiping with us on Sundays, we need to meet them where they are Monday through Saturday.

Here's our game plan:

In part 1, we'll talk about what *it* is and why we need to lead like it matters.

In part 2, we'll explore the seven leadership principles for a church that lasts. But I'll do a deeper dive into what has changed and how we need to think differently, and raise the questions we will work together to answer.

Then in part 3, I'm excited to expand into new areas I didn't have a clue mattered years ago. I'll introduce and unpack three important realms of leadership every church leader must master to lead like *it* matters and maximize their ministry's God-given potential:

1. Why we need to prioritize mindset over model.
2. How to create systems that empower *it*.
3. A balanced way to lead so you stay centered around *it*.

It has been said, "The church is the hope of the world." Some sincere and well-meaning Christians push back, explaining that technically, Jesus is the hope of the world. While I'll never argue against the importance of the risen Son of God, I believe strongly in the power of Jesus *through* the church. After all, the church is the body of Christ. Jesus manifested himself through the church. The church is not a place we go. The church is who we are. And we are chosen and called by God to be light in the darkness and to give hope to the hopeless. More than anything, I want to help you lead like *it* matters.

If you believe God wants to use you in his church and as his church, read on. As you do, read prayerfully. If possible, don't read alone. Invite friends from your small group, church staff, or church leadership team to join you.

If you believe God wants to use your church to glorify himself and make a difference in this world, let's seek him together. Keep an open mind, be alert to his prompting, and believe by faith that he will hear the cries of your heart and move freely and powerfully through your church. If you are ready for your church to understand what *it* is and why it matters, and to unleash it to make an eternal difference, then this is my prayer for you:

Heavenly Father, thank you for every spiritual leader who loves your bride, the church. I pray, God, that you will give each pastor, each leader, each volunteer a renewed love for the gospel, an overwhelming burden for those who don't know Jesus, and an unstoppable passion to unleash the power of the church to transform the world.

Build the faith of each person who is reading this book, because I know you want to do more in them and through them than they ever believed possible. Silence the distracting and discouraging voice of the enemy. Quench the lies that immobilize your spiritual army. Burn away spiritual apathy with a fire for holiness, truth, and transformed lives.

Replace our apathy with passion from heaven.

Transform fear into a burning faith.

Renew our love for those who don't know Jesus.

Empower your church to meet the needs of the broken.

Bring dead churches back to life with your resurrection power.

When the world grows darker, help the light of your church grow brighter.

All that the world might know Jesus and glorify you, Father.

In Jesus' name, amen.

Introduction

S ome ministries have *it*. Some don't.

Most churches want *it*. Few have it.

The good news is that when a church has *it*, everyone knows it. But when one doesn't—well, everyone knows that too.

The same is true with pastors and leaders. Some have *it*. Some don't. It is obvious when someone has it and when someone doesn't.

It is always unique. It is always powerful. It is always life-changing.

That's *it's* upside. *It* has another side too. It attracts critics. It is controversial. Many people misunderstand it. It is hard to find, but it is impossible to miss.

By now you're probably asking, *What is it?* My answer is . . .

I don't know.

Really, I don't.

It is hard to define because you can't see it. But unlike the Loch Ness Monster, Bigfoot, or a mermaid riding a unicorn, it is real.

So what is it?

I don't know.

Here's what I do know: if you've ever been involved in a ministry that had *it*, you had this sense you were part of something special. Though you probably couldn't describe *it*, you still knew it when you saw it. It was an indescribable work of God that could not be explained or contained.

If you've never seen *it* up close, ask around and see if you can find it. Just listen to what people around you are saying. I promise, if a ministry or church near you gets *it,* people will be talking about it. When a ministry has *it,* there's electricity in the air, the ground seems to rumble. Everyone becomes aware of it. You'll see it on social media. People will talk about it at the office. Your friends will tell you they heard about it from their friends. "You have to visit this church. I've never seen anything like it. What's going on there is incredible. Trust me. It will blow your mind. I promise you will love it."

Because of the buzz, people flock to check out churches that have *it.* Not only do they kick the tires, many of them actually join. Not only do they join, many get obsessed with the ministry and throw their whole hearts and lives into it. They seem to intuitively grasp whatever *it* is. They can't get enough of it.

To an outsider with a critical heart, these converts simply drank the Kool-Aid and became fanatics. But to those who experience *it,* life is different. They become a passionate part of a movement. They are changed by being caught up in something only God can do.

They are so excited, they want everyone to know about *it.*

If you're still not sure what I'm talking about, this book should shed some light on *it.* You might be thinking, *But I don't understand. Aren't some people just born with it while others never find it?* Without a doubt, *it* is always and only a gift from God. But I believe God makes it available to anyone who wants it. I believe he wants to give it to you and your ministry. And I believe you can learn to lead like *it* matters. That may be difficult for you to imagine, but it's true.

To be clear, I will share what I have learned in more than twenty-six years of leading our church, but I'm not going to give you a plug-and-play formula. We will look at seven factors that contribute to *it* (or at least don't kill it):

1. Vision
2. Divine focus
3. Unmistakable camaraderie
4. Innovative minds
5. Willingness to fall short
6. Hearts focused outward
7. Kingdom-mindedness

While I can't promise *it* to you, I can tell you that those seven leadership principles will lead you toward it. And I can help you lead like *it* matters. After walking through the seven factors, we will discover three simple, combustible principles that will help you lead like *it* matters and can ignite it in your heart, life, and church.

I'm praying the ministry you love will find *it*.

And never lose it.

PART 1

WHAT IS *IT*?

CHAPTER 1

Some Have *It*, Some Don't

The perfect church service would be one we were almost unaware of. Our attention would have been on God.

—C. S. Lewis

I was a beer-drinking, girl-chasing, hell-raising frat boy. Then I was a Jesus freak.

I became a Christ follower midway through college. I was walking on campus when someone handed me a free Gideon Bible. I had gone to church but had little to no faith and had never dug into the Bible. I decided to read it, and it was like nothing I had read before. I met Jesus through that little green free Bible and decided I wanted to spend the rest of my life following him.

Even as a brand-new believer, I knew I had to find a church.

How do you find a church? I had no idea. I assumed churches were pretty much all the same, so I wasn't too worried about it. Being saved was important, but so was saving gas money, so I went looking for the church closest to my college campus.

Pretty quickly, I found it! A gorgeous, genuinely historical church. It had *everything:* stained-glass windows, a mile-high steeple, and best of all, a huge bell. (I had no idea why a church needed a bell, but still, I was impressed. Even to this day I suffer from a bit of bell envy.)

I did my best to make a good first impression at my potential church home. I didn't own a suit, so I wore my nicest khakis, my braided leather belt, shiny penny loafers, and a wrinkly white shirt (no tie), with my hair perfectly parted down the middle and feathered on the sides. (Give me a break. It was the eighties.) I looked like I had walked straight off the set of *Miami Vice*, except, of course, I was wearing socks. (And didn't live in a houseboat with an alligator named Elvis, though that was part of my ten-year plan.)

I remember climbing up the front stairs of one of the most gorgeous historic churches in our city. The climb seemed endless, heading for the massive, perfectly carved wooden doors. (I won't even tell you about my door envy.) The bouncer at the door (I now know churches don't call that dude a bouncer) looked like he'd just eaten a bowl of horseradish. He glared at me with disapproval. Maybe it was because I had skipped the tie, hadn't ironed my clothes, and wasn't carrying a Bible. In any case, I didn't feel welcome.

I was already nervous, and his not-so-friendly greeting heightened my uneasiness. My next greeting was inside, where bouncer number two seemed to look me up and down suspiciously. I was paranoid and assumed he was gauging whether he should waste one of his bulletins on me. Evidently, I was bulletin worthy. But just barely.

Clutching my treasure, I walked reverently into the beautiful, mostly empty sanctuary. Since I didn't want to be tardy my first time, I had arrived several minutes before the service was scheduled to start. I assumed it was empty because the crowd would show up precisely on time.

A few people mingled, but no one said hello to me—or to anyone else they didn't know.

A couple of congregants were already seated, scattered around here and there, alone. I took my cue from them and found a seat. A minute later, a sour-faced, white-haired woman told me that I was in her seat. (I wondered whether a section of wooden bench could even be called a seat, whether she had first claimed this "seat" in 1879, and why she couldn't just sit in one of the four vacant rows nearby.) Instead of claiming squatter's rights, I sheepishly got up and found a new place to sit. It wasn't hard. The place was nearly empty.

The crowd never showed.

Finally, a man in a religious robe sauntered regally to the podium and with arms outstretched offered us, in a very pastoral voice, "Greetings in the name of the Lord." Everyone mumbled something I couldn't understand and stood up almost as one, and the organ sputtered to life. We sang three hymns like we were lifeless robots.

For each hymn, we sang verses one, two, and four. What did they have against verse three? Had someone abducted all of the verse threes? Had they notified the proper authorities?

After the songs, another guy in a robe came up, less regally, and droned some announcements. I think a women's quilting circle was mentioned, but I couldn't be sure because I was lost in his monotone voice. Finally, we came to the feature presentation. The guy with the nicest, fanciest robe—I assumed he was the senior pastor (making the other two junior pastors?)—got up to deliver a sermon that would feed our hungry souls. He talked. And he talked and he talked. And unfortunately, I stayed hungry.

When he finally finished, everyone got up and left unceremoniously. I dutifully followed the flow of traffic out the door and got in my car. On my drive home, I was bewildered, struggling to understand why God—this God who had so radically transformed my life with his irresistible grace and unfathomable power, who breathed into me new life and new passion—would demand that I waste my Sunday mornings like this.

Looking back, I know these were faithful church members who

never intended to send an uncaring message. But good intentions don't always translate into a good and healthy church community.

I left having no idea what *it* is but knowing I had just experienced its absence. And I figured, if that beautiful, majestic church didn't have *it*, what hope did I have of finding it in any other church?

> Good intentions don't always translate into a good and healthy church community.

Can You Feel It in the Air Tonight?

I still remember that experience vividly. No one was friendly. No one smiled. No one told me they were glad I had visited. No one invited me back. No one seemed excited about anything. It was as if the church had died years before, but no one had noticed.

I returned to my college campus disappointed and a little confused. I went to the cafeteria for lunch. I was distracted from eating our cafeteria's sad version of a wannabe corn dog by a boisterous group of about twenty students that came in laughing, cutting up, and talking over each other—and carrying Bibles!

I watched them carefully, trying not to stare. They prayed before they ate. But they didn't just "say grace." They really *prayed*. With sincerity. For an uncomfortably long time.

As they began eating, their relational electricity resumed. When I couldn't hold back my curiosity anymore, I got up and walked in their direction. As I approached, one guy's head whipped around toward me and a broad smile spread across his face. He sprang up and lunged toward me with his hand extended. "Is it true? Is it true? We heard . . . Did you *really* find Christ?"

Though we'd never met before, evidently, he'd heard about my newfound faith. We bonded instantly. His eyes welled up with tears as he told me that he and others had been praying for more than a year for me to come to Christ. I was stunned. Speechless. Humbled.

Blown away. And overwhelmed with gratitude. *Someone has been praying? For me? How did they know? I've been hurting so badly. I've been so far from God, so desperate. Searching for something, anything. How did they know?*

He invited me to join them and introduced me to everyone at the table. These people were different. Passionate, godly, sincere, authentic, transparent, hungry for Christ. They had something different. They had *it*. And it was instantly recognizable. It was too obvious to miss.

After just a few minutes, they invited me to come to church with them—that same night. Like me, most of them had just come from church. How could someone possibly *want* to go to church twice in one day? How could anyone get past those grumpy guys with irritable bouncer syndrome twice in one day?

> **P**assionate, godly, sincere, authentic, transparent, hungry for Christ. They had something different. They had *it*.

Yet they wanted to go—again. I found out later the reason was that their church had *it*. And what they had was contagious.

They insisted that I dress casually, so when I met them later, I was wearing my OP shorts and my favorite blue T-shirt. (If you don't know, OP stands for Ocean Pacific. OP was a third-level brand on the cool scale. Third-level-brand cool was barely acceptable. A distinct level below Izods and two levels below the prized Polos.) Clutching my shiny, green, crisp, pocket-sized Gideon New Testament, I crammed into the car with several others as they rocked out the Pioneer stereo to a Christian group called Petra.

As we approached their church, I was confused. It didn't make sense. The building didn't look like a church. It wasn't pretty at all. No steps. No steeple. No stained glass. And absolutely no bell. It was just a plain metal structure. Actually, calling it plain is generous. It was ugly. Like "U-G-L-Y, you ain't got no alibi" ugly.

Since traffic was backed up for half a block, we had to wait a long time, but no one seemed to mind or even notice. Old people, young people, rich people, poor people, every kind of people from every ethnic and economic background excitedly made their way inside. When we finally parked the car and headed in, I was swarmed by smiling people warmly welcoming me. One guy even gave me a hug. He had obviously failed church-bouncer school, which the two grumpy old men from that morning had aced.

Inside, nothing about this building was special. Even if there had been something worth noticing, I would have missed it because of all the people.

They were everywhere.

It was also *loud*. Imagine a packed lobby crammed with teen-agers waiting for a Bieber concert. That's kind of what it felt like. But instead of drugs and alcohol like you'd see at most parties or concerts, I found warm smiles, contagious laughter, loving hugs, and Bibles everywhere. The room was electric. The fire marshal probably would have had a stroke if he had seen it. But everyone was too excited to notice and too passionate to care.

And that was just the lobby.

Get Ready for *It*

Something special was about to happen. Everyone knew it. More than just anticipating it, they were positively expecting it. I'd had no idea what would happen when I agreed to come, but now I was expecting it too. Even as a first-time visitor, I could sense something significant was about to go down.

We were still in the lobby when music started to come through a double doorway. Like a pack of hungry piranha, this swarm of people rushed in. We rode the wave into . . . What would you call a big room like that? A sanctuary? An auditorium? A multipurpose room? A great place for a killer game of dodgeball? With its contagiously exciting atmosphere, it didn't really matter what you called it.

People there loved God, and they were ecstatic to have the opportunity to express their hearts. Some cried. Some lifted their hands. (*What's that about?* I wondered.) Some shouted. Some danced. Some knelt in prayer.

When the preacher walked up to speak, he had something about him that was hard to describe. He seemed confident, but it was so much more. Somehow he was confident *and* humble at the same time. He seemed to be glowing. It was as if he'd just gotten off a FaceTime call with God, and God had given him a message to share with us. He smiled knowingly with spiritual assurance.

As the preacher began to preach, people leaned in, listening intently, as if every word mattered. To me every word did matter. His message pierced my heart as though he were speaking directly to me. It felt like I was the only person in the room. To this day, more than thirty years later, I remember certain details of that message. (That's saying a lot, because I often forget what I preached last week.) His message impacted me. The church impacted me. The people impacted me. Really, through it all, God impacted me.

When I met Christ, I became a different person. Forgiven. Transformed. New. I now had *two* momentous moments—being saved, and experiencing God at that church. It was another turning point. I came back again and again, multiple times a week. I started to serve, to invite others, and even to tithe. As a result, I experienced God in a new and deeper way. My desire for him wasn't about what he could do for me. It was for him and nothing else. From that day forward I was somehow a different person. God was no longer just someone who did something for me. I was overwhelmed with an awareness that it was about my loving him. It was about his will. His plan. His desire to reach other people—through me.

God was no longer just someone who did something for me.

This church had *it*.
I wanted it.
I needed it.
And I got it.

It Factors

- Beautiful buildings, cool environments, and the right technology aren't necessary to have *it*.
- A person surrendered fully to Christ gets *it*.
- Once a person has *it*, he can't keep it to himself.

Questions for Discussion or Reflection

1. Have you ever visited a church that had everything and yet didn't have *it*? What happened? How did you feel? What can you learn from those experiences?
2. Think about people you know who have *it*. Describe what it is about them that is contagious.
3. Sometimes when another ministry has *it*, a natural response to not understanding *it* is to become critical of it. What ministry do you know of that has *it*? What do you think they do that contributes to it? What do you think you could learn from them?
4. Every ministry has strengths and weaknesses. How does your ministry excel? What part of your ministry is best helping people get *it*? What part of your ministry needs to be developed to better help people experience *it*?

CHAPTER 2

Where Did *It* Come From?

The wind blows wherever it pleases. You hear its sound, but you cannot tell where it comes from or where it is going. So it is with everyone born of the Spirit.

—Jesus (John 3:8)

For years, I've been intrigued by *it*.

My appreciation for *it* started at that Sunday night service when I had my first taste of it. After that night in the presence of God at church, I couldn't get enough of it. Getting involved at that church wrecked me in the best sort of way and redirected the trajectory of my life. I knew I had to become a pastor. This wasn't a career change. This was a calling. I felt called, compelled, and chosen by God to give my life to him serving in his church.

Shortly after that in 1991, I became an associate pastor of First United Methodist Church in downtown Oklahoma City. This historic and more traditional church had aged along with the community. But after a change in leadership, the new pastor, Nick Harris (who is in heaven now), slowly started making some changes. At first, many people resisted his ideas. Some members left quickly. A few new ones joined.

Pastor Nick started a Bible study for downtown business leaders. At first, only a handful came for a free sandwich and a hearty Bible lesson. Over time, though, a couple of influential business leaders got excited about Jesus and invited their employees to this Bible study. Before long, several people came to faith in Christ and rumors spread around downtown. Something was happening during lunch at the old Methodist church down the street.

The new believers got baptized. They invited friends and family to the Bible study. The study exploded, and then people made their way to the weekend worship services.

Suddenly the Sunday services, which had been predictable and quiet, showed signs of spiritual life. Attendance grew. Ministry impact expanded. Church membership exploded. Lives were changed.

It didn't happen overnight. But it did happen. The church that didn't have *it* got it.

No one could deny it.

During my five years there, the church doubled in size. Business leaders were continually coming to faith in Christ. The new single-adults ministry quickly grew to become the largest in the state. We baptized hundreds of people. God was glorified.

The church that doesn't have *it* can get it.

Even after my pastor retired and another pastor stepped in, the spiritual momentum didn't wane. The church continued to enjoy *it* for close to a decade.

Then one day, *it* started to fade. No one noticed it at first. Based on my experience, people rarely do. But like a tire with a slow and almost unnoticeable leak, *it* started to diminish. Fewer people came to Christ. Passionate prayer meetings became less passionate and then less of a priority. The once-powerful single-adults ministry now hung on by a thread. Some of the people who were the most excited in years past left to go to other churches. Instead of never missing a week of church, many people missed often and eventually stopped coming altogether.

Sadly, this church doesn't have *it* anymore.

After having watched the church be blessed with *it*, many people mourn that that same church is now, years later, struggling without it.

You could say "*it* happens."

But not always.

When You Least Expect It

In 1996, Pokemon was introduced to the world, Fox News Channel made its debut, Bill Clinton was reelected president of the United States, and my wife, Amy, and I started Life.Church. (I'm guessing you don't remember the launch of Life.Church. Again, no offense taken.)

In those early years, we didn't have anything most churches have (and think are necessary). We had almost nothing. What we did have was junk.

We met in a borrowed two-car garage that smelled just like a garage. (You may have noticed there are no Musty Garage Breeze air fresheners at the store.)

On the first weekend of our new church, we experienced a rare Oklahoma snowstorm. I still remember people wearing their winter hats and gloves, huddling together for the entire service to stay warm.

Since I knew the importance of caring for kids, we reserved the best facilities for children under five years of age. They met for children's church in a large storage closet. That's right! Only the best for our kids.

We had one temperamental microphone and two borrowed

karaoke speakers. We borrowed seventy-five green, felt-backed chairs from hell. (All felt-backed chairs are from hell and should be returned there as soon as possible.) The garage was so dark we bought a floodlight from the hardware store for $19.99 to light it. This innovation worked great until one day the light exploded during the middle of the worship service. People thought terrorists were attacking and dove for cover. (On a positive note, several people accepted Christ that day for fear it was their last.)

Today, Life.Church is often known for leveraging technology to reach and minister to people whenever possible. In the early days, we were excited if something we plugged in didn't blow up, including our hand-me-down early-1970s overhead projector.

For those of you who don't know what an overhead projector is, I'll explain. An overhead projector was the state-of-the-art, cutting-edge way (in 1976; unfortunately, this was 1996) to display song lyrics on a screen. Or in our case, on a garage door.

To use the overhead projector—commonly referred to simply as "the overhead"—you'd write or type the words on a sheet of transparent plastic, place the sheet on the bed of the projector, and voila! Worship magic.

In churches today, you often have people serve in the kids' ministry, as small group leaders, on the student ministry team, or as ushers. (You've got to have the spiritual gift of ushing.) Back in 1996, one of the most important volunteer roles in the church was the overhead-projector-transparency flipper. This person had to have impeccable timing. As the congregation sang, the OPTF had to anticipate the flow of the Spirit and remove the transparency from the projector at precisely the right moment. Without losing a second, the OPTF quickly replaced that transparency with the next one, displaying the lyrics to the next worship song. (To keep it manageable, we always skipped verse 3. Verses 1, 2, and 4 only. Got to stick with tradition.) If this sounds complicated, believe me, it was.

Our OPTF was Jerome. Jerome was a new Christian who had lost a finger to a gunshot wound in a drug deal gone bad. (Yes, the drug thing was before he became a Christian. But he was still new to his Christian faith and rough around the edges. I'm convinced that for a hundred dollars, Jerome would have made anyone disappear for me.) Whenever someone new attended our garage church, they would be mesmerized by the light shining onto the garage door, then let their gaze follow the light to its source, where they beheld Jerome's hand and silently counted his fingers: one, two, three, four . . . Four?

Exquisite Intensity

Why am I telling you all of this? Well, it's cheaper than counseling. But I also want you to understand we didn't have anything most people think you need to have church.

Depending on your church background, you likely think some things are necessary to have a great church worship experience. Whatever you think you need, we didn't have that.

We didn't have a nice building. We didn't have our own offices. We didn't have a phone number (unless you count my home phone number). We didn't have a paid staff. We didn't have a logo. We didn't have a website. We didn't serve Starbucks. We didn't have an organ. We didn't have a choir with robes or a rock band with guys wearing skinny jeans and sporting lots of hair product. We didn't have candles to spark the mood or a laser light show that pierced through the smoke from the fog machines. We didn't have hymnals or sermon series with titles copied from the most popular Netflix shows.

What did we have? We had a few people; you could count them on both hands. (Well, Jerome couldn't, but you could.) Those few people were off-the-charts excited about Jesus. We had enough Bibles to go around. And we had *it*.

At the time, I didn't call it *it*.

But we were definitely full of it.

Even though we didn't know what it was, we knew it was from God. And it was special.

Whatever *it* was, everyone felt it. They talked about it. New people came and experienced it. The church grew. And grew. And grew. Lives were changed by the dozens. Then by the hundreds. Then by the thousands.

E**ven though we didn't know what it was, we knew it was from God. And it was special.**

Twenty-five years later, we are known as the largest attended church in the history of North America. As of today, we are meeting in more than forty locations in more than a dozen different states.

But about a decade into our ministry, I noticed something that gave me pause. Over time, it made me nervous. Finally, it bothered me deeply and kept me awake at night.

In some of our church locations, we were losing *it*.

Even though I had never known what caused *it*, I had always hoped we'd never lose it. Yet we were.

Although many of our churches unquestionably still had *it*, in other locations, we had to admit that it seemed to have quit. That distinct spiritual hum, so obvious before, was harder to hear. The once-unmistakable spiritual passion of so many people started to wane. The life-changing stories that were once a part of every discussion came fewer and farther between.

Instead of passionately caring about people who didn't know Christ, some members started to gripe about how the church wasn't all they wanted it to be. Instead of people coming early and staying late, they came late and often left early. Instead of begging their friends to join them for church, they frequently skipped themselves. Instead of sacrificing for the cause of Christ, people appeared to be consuming, not contributing.

I started to lose sleep. Night after night I lay in bed, staring at the ceiling, asking . . .

Where did *it* go?

Why did we lose it?

Did we kill it?

Did God take it away?

Random It-ness

In the past, I figured if a church didn't have *it,* it was, at least to some extent, the leadership's fault. The elders must not have been focused or passionate or praying or fasting, or maybe they were secretly sinning. If it wasn't the church leadership, it must have been the senior pastor's fault. Surely the senior pastor hadn't cast a compelling Christ-focused vision, or he didn't preach hard enough or wasn't inspiring people to become like Christ. Or maybe it was the staff's problem. Perhaps the staff had gotten tired, bored, or lazy.

Surely someone was to blame.

That was easy to believe until *we* had a problem.

For us, diagnosing the problem was complicated. Why? All of our church campuses were almost identical, but the results were dramatically different.

All of our buildings are designed to have a similar look and feel. If we blindfolded you and took you to any Life.Church location, then removed your blindfold, you would have no idea which city you were in. You could be in Albany or Fort Worth or Kansas City or Colorado Springs and you wouldn't know unless you stepped outside the building.

We work hard to cultivate exactly the same values, culture, and leadership on every church campus. We hire every staff member through exactly the same strategic process. The teams from every campus are trained together, centrally, the same way every time.

Each weekend, the people attending in every church location hear the same message. The worship pastors are unique but sing the same songs with a consistent style.

The kids' curriculum never varies from church campus to church campus. All the kids at every campus have the same experiences in different environments.

Sure, some of our campus pastors are more seasoned leaders than others. And we understood that ministering in different cities and states produces somewhat different outcomes. Yet the difference in results was too dramatic to overlook. Some Life.Church campuses had *it*. Others didn't. That's when we started officially calling it *it*.

We couldn't ignore the fact that some church campuses had huge numbers of people coming to faith in Jesus, while others struggled to lead anyone to Christ. Those campuses with many people coming to Christ always seemed to have more than enough engaged and committed volunteers. The others often struggled to fill a minimum quota.

At the with-*it* church campuses, people seemed naturally to grow in their generosity to the church and outside the church. The *it*-less campuses were financially stagnant.

One church campus tripled in size in one year, while growth in others was flat. Two grew to more than two thousand people in a year. That same year, one shrank.

Guess which one shrank? The answer might surprise you. If you aren't familiar with multisite churches, they come in all different shapes, models, styles, and sizes. At our church, we have one broadcast location. Each week, a pastor preaches from the broadcast location, which sends the message live over satellite to all the others. Naturally, people would assume that the one with the in-person preacher would always be full and growing. In 2008, the only Life.Church location that got smaller was the one where I taught in person. That's right. All the church campuses that watched the message on video grew that year. The one where I was didn't. (If you don't like video teaching, put that in your pipe and smoke it.)

Why did some church locations have *it*? Why did others not? Most of all, why did the one where I preached lose it? What happened to the passion, the intensity, the buzz, and the spiritual momentum we'd enjoyed for close to a decade?

As I dug into this problem, I realized that not only did the church campuses have varying degrees of *it* but individual teams did too. To support our campuses around the nation, we have a central organization divided into dozens of teams with several hundred employees total. We noticed that some teams had that something special—that energy, drive, oomph—while others didn't. The same was true at a church location. The student ministry might have *it* but the missions team didn't.

As we tried to get our minds around it, we began thinking about other churches around the nation. I realized I could name a dozen that used to have *it,* but not anymore. At one time, they were reaching tons of people, growing with cutting-edge ministry innovations. People would travel across town or even across the country to see what God was doing there. Church leaders would study these ministries, often attempting to copy them. But somewhere along the journey, they seemed to freeze in time, then slowly thaw and melt away.

They once had *it*. They lost it.

Could that be happening to us?

I watched a few other churches whose growth had been flat for years. But one day, something changed. Maybe they got a new leader. Or their leader found a second wind. Perhaps God gave a staff member an idea that worked. I don't know, it could be that they redecorated the church building in God's favorite color. (If so, I wanted to know: What is God's favorite color?!) Whatever the reasons, I could think of many churches that didn't have *it* for years but then got it. Sudden, dramatic resuscitation.

Two important principles, or It Factors, dawned on me:

It Factors

- The good news: if you don't have *it*, you can get it.
- The bad news: if you have *it*, you can lose it.

Questions for Discussion or Reflection

1. If a church lacks what most people think you need to have church, yet they have *it*, does this mean that buildings, environments, logos, websites, and so on are not important? Why or why not?
2. Can you think of an example of a church that had *it* and then lost it? Describe what happened. Why do you think that ministry lost it?
3. If you've ever been part of a ministry that had *it*, you knew it. Describe what it felt like. What were some of the qualities that you experienced and appreciated?
4. What part of your ministry has *it*? (Your choir, student ministry, or hospitality ministry might have it.) What factors do you believe contribute to it?

CHAPTER 3

Bringing *It* into Focus

Leadership is like beauty. It's hard to define, but you know it when you see it.

—Warren Bennis

I t wasn't just the sauce.

Amy was so godly, so fun, so smart, so . . . beautiful that I'm sure I would have fallen in love with her and married her anyway, but man, the sauce sure did help seal the deal.

As a new Christian in college, I started hearing "you're weird" and "you're a Jesus freak" kinds of comments. One day someone said, "You should meet Amy—she's weird like you." We met and she wasn't just "Jesus weird," she was amazing. The only thing I can compare to her is the sauce.

It was one of our first dates. Amy invited me over for dinner. I arrived to discover she had made spaghetti and marinara sauce. Okay, sounds good. I liked spaghetti just fine. We sat down and I tasted the sauce.

Mind.

Blown.

I had eaten spaghetti sauce before, probably a hundred times, but this was different. What made it different? I don't know. I couldn't adequately describe it, but I knew I had never tasted anything like it. I knew I wanted more of it. And I knew I wasn't letting go of anyone who could make something that tasted this good. Amy was a keeper!

I can't tell you exactly what it is. Part of what makes it *it* is that it defies categorization. It won't reduce to a memorable slogan. It is far too special for that.

That's why we have to embrace the fact that God makes *it* happen. It is from him. It is by him. It is for his glory. We can't create it. We can't reproduce it. We can't manufacture it.

We have to embrace the fact that God makes *it* happen.

It is not a model. It is not a style. It is not the result of a program. You can't purchase it or assemble it. It can't be copied.

Not everyone will get *it*. It can't be learned in a classroom. Yet even though it can't be taught, it can be caught.

Good News about *It*

Here's some good news about *it:* you can find it in all types of churches. It is in traditional churches, contemporary churches, charismatic churches, seeker-sensitive churches, emergent churches, and submergent churches. (Okay, I made up that last category.) You can find it in rural communities, in suburbs, in big cities, and in underground churches in countries where it's illegal to meet for corporate worship. It is in nondenominational churches, Assembly of God churches, Evangelical Covenant churches, Baptist churches, Bible churches, Lutheran churches, Methodist churches, and Episcopalian churches.

Even though you can find *it* in all of those places, you can also go to thousands of these same types of churches that don't have it.

But whenever God gives it to you, it is unmistakable.

Based on my experience as a pastor and leadership student, here are some observations I can offer you about it.

When *It* Works

When a ministry has *it*, most things the leaders try seem to work.

If the church sends out an invitational mailer, new people come—and stick. If they post sermon clips on their Instagram account, lots of people engage. If they write worship songs, people can't wait to download them and rush to church to sing them. If they brainstorm about taking on a local missions project, people line up to get involved and the community changes for the better. If a global pandemic closes the doors to the church, these passionate Christ followers move their ministry exclusively online and continue to make a difference.

When a ministry has *it,* the staff know they're part of something much bigger than themselves. They are important players participating in a divine mission, an unstoppable force, flowing with contagious passion. They show up early for almost everything. They often stay late. They rarely fight. When they disagree, they grow through their differences, usually quickly.

When a church has *it,* creativity flows. Everyone comes up with ideas, and those ideas just seem to change lives.

On the other hand, when a ministry doesn't have *it,* most of what they try doesn't work. When they send an invitational mailer, few people come to church as a result and even fewer return. When they start a new contemporary worship service, it putts along for six months or so, then kaput. When they launch a social media campaign, it flounders. If they write worship music, the songs don't catch on. If they attempt a local missions project, they have to cancel it for lack of interest. And when a global pandemic hits, the ministry stalls and the people seem to scatter.

A ministry that doesn't have *it* simply follows the formula they used the year before and the year before that. People are bored, uninspired, and complacent.

When a church doesn't have *it,* the staff is simply doing a job, drawing a paycheck, passing time. They're territorial. Jealous. Dissatisfied. Discontented. Even bitter.

Knowing *It*

I've noticed that when a church doesn't have *it,* few people seem to even notice. They don't seem to realize that no one new is showing up. It's certainly not a cause for alarm. Mostly they're just committed to and comfortable with the status quo.

When a church does have *it,* everyone knows it. They can feel it, though they would have trouble describing it. Everyone recognizes it, but no one knows precisely what it is.

> When a church does have *it,* everyone knows it.

It's a lot like the first-century church you read about in the book of Acts. They unquestionably had *it.* Think about the astounding works of God recorded in Scripture. No human could have created all that *it.*

Peter—who had been a bumbling and chronically inconsistent failure—preached, and three thousand people were saved, baptized, and filled with the Spirit of God (Acts 2:41). When the church was persecuted and believers were tortured and often killed, the church, instead of shrinking, grew! If a person had a need, someone sold their possessions to meet that need. If a Christian was arrested for preaching about Jesus, he would just worship God in prison or lead the jailer to Christ. Occasionally, God would even break him out of jail. One time, Paul's sermon went long, and a drowsy kid drifted off, fell from a second-story window, and was pronounced dead. Paul just raised him back to life. That's some pretty cool *it!*

The first church had *it*. They didn't create it. God did. But they worked with it. And they made sure not to get in its way.

I love how they're described in Acts 2:43: "Everyone kept feeling a sense of awe" (NASB). They didn't know what *it* was, but they knew they had it.

Getting *It*

At this point, you may be thinking, *We don't have it, but we want it. How do we get it?*

You may fear it's not possible. Back in 1992, En Vogue sang, "No, you're never gonna get it. Never ever gonna get it." They were talking about a very different kind of it, but you might feel like they're singing to you. You realize that your ministry doesn't have *it,* and you want it, but you're not sure if that's possible, and if it is, *how* do you get it?

What I've found is that leaders in churches without *it* often try to manufacture it. Problem: it cannot be manufactured.

You can lead like *it* matters, but you can't create it. How might leaders try to do that? Someone might visit a growing church and observe outward signs of success—videos, buildings, fancy kids' rooms, a certain style of music, and so on. These well-meaning guests mistakenly think, *That's why they have* it. *If we had all that, we'd have it too.*

You can lead like *it* matters, but you can't create it. They couldn't be more wrong.

The first-century church in Jerusalem clearly had *it*. Yet they didn't have any of these fancy accoutrements. No historic cathedrals. No professionally produced video roll-ins to the latest four-part sermon series. No climbing walls in the youth wing or LED walls in the auditorium.

Fast-forward to 1996. Our church in a garage had *it*. Yet if you came, the only thing that might have impressed you is that a guy with four fingers could deftly handle overhead transparencies. Perhaps you would have left thinking, *If we could just get our own four-fingered tech volunteer, maybe . . .* No. Just like with the church in Jerusalem, you would have seen no physical, external factors that were producing success.

So *it* can't possibly be stained-glass windows, handcarved cherubs, custom-made silk tapestries, gold-inlaid hymnals, thousand-pipe organs, marble floors, mile-high steeples, handpainted ceilings, mahogany pews, giant cast-iron bells, and three-piece, thousand-dollar suits. *It* doesn't stick any better to a young, hip pastor with tattoos and overpriced kicks than it does to an older, stately gentleman in a robe. Nor is *it* spotlights and lasers, video production, satellite dishes, fog machines, shiny gauze backdrops, four-color glossy brochures, creative billboards, loud contemporary music, free donuts, coffee shops, hip bookstores, break dancing or acrobatics, sermon series based on movies, or a retro-modern matching chair and table onstage. *It* is not being on television, streaming on YouTube, speaking at conferences, having your own leadership podcast, or doing Instagram Live with the hottest celebrities.

You might be thinking, *C'mon. Aren't the churches that have it the churches that have supercharismatic speakers or turbocharged spiritual leaders? Doesn't it show up at churches led by ten-talent people?*

I will admit, such leaders can draw a crowd. They can create ministries that look like they have *it*. But don't be fooled by imitations (or *it*mitations). If a church's success is based merely on a gifted leader trying to fabricate *it*, that ministry is built on sand and will not last. It cannot be sustained by human talent.

So again, what is *it* and, more important, how do you get it?

To answer, can I take you back to my wife's marinara sauce? I had never tasted anything so good. Ask me why. Ask me what made it so delicious. I don't know. I don't, but my wife does. She would tell you it isn't any one thing; it is the right combination of some essential ingredients. She makes the sauce from a recipe that has been handed down from generation to generation among her ancestors in Eastern Europe. As you might expect, the recipe calls for tomatoes and garlic and oregano. You might be surprised to learn that the recipe includes bell peppers and carrots. And—are you ready for this—there is bacon in this sauce! You thought I was exaggerating when I said it is the best sauce ever. No. It has bacon!

So forget spaghetti sauce. (Though it is hard to forget.) Let's talk about *it:* What is it and how do you get it? I don't know. But God does. And I think he would tell you it's not one thing. It's the right combination of some essential ingredients. You can develop it from the recipe he's handed down from generation to generation from those first Christians we read about in the book of Acts.

As we studied our church campuses that had *it*, we realized they consistently had seven key ingredients. The campuses that didn't have *it* were missing several of these ingredients. As I've observed churches and ministries around the world, the ones that have these factors have *it*. The ones that don't, don't.

It is what God does through a rare combination of these qualities found in his people and in his church:

1. Vision
2. Divine focus
3. Unmistakable camaraderie
4. Innovative minds
5. Willingness to fall short
6. Hearts focused outward
7. Kingdom-mindedness

Good news: you can develop these qualities. Bad news: spiritual shortcuts rarely work. That's why it would be stupid for me to write a book guaranteeing "Three Steps to Get *It*."

But what I can do is give you clarity on these qualities. That's what we're going to do in part 2 of this book. We will carefully and prayerfully look at the ingredients in this recipe so we have clarity on what they are and can ask God to grow them in us and in our ministries.

Then in part 3, we'll learn how to lead like *it* matters. We'll see how *it* comes not from a model but from a mindset, how to create systems that facilitate it, and how to become a centered leader who has it.

Some of our journey will be fun and encouraging. You'll have moments of celebration as God affirms that you've been following his leading.

At other times, you may find yourself challenged, perhaps painfully so. You might even get mad at me. That's okay. That's all part of the journey to *it*. I hope to push you. Disturb you. Stretch you.

If you don't already see *it* in your ministry, perhaps it is closer than you think, bubbling just beneath the surface.

Maybe it's time to boil.

It Factors

- *It* is not a model, system, or result of programs.
- You cannot purchase *it*. It can't be copied.
- Not everyone will get *it*.
- *It* cannot be learned. Even though it can't be taught, it can be caught.
- *It* happens when we allow God to grow certain vital characteristics in us and in the ministries we lead.

Questions for Discussion or Reflection

1. *It* can be found in all types of churches. Do you agree or disagree? Why?
2. What *it* is not can be fairly obvious. What do you think are some ways of describing what *it* isn't?
3. In the next section of the book, we will discuss qualities that contribute to *it*. Before you look ahead, make a list of a few factors you think contribute to it.
4. What have you focused on that you thought would bring *it* but now you recognize won't? What can you do about it?

PART 2

WHAT CONTRIBUTES TO *IT?*

I live in Oklahoma, where college football is everything. The Oklahoma Sooners often win their division, occasionally competing for the national championship. In 2019, Oklahoma made the Bowl Championship Series, again, and met a wrecking ball in the LSU Tigers. LSU beat Oklahoma 63–28 on their way to an undefeated championship season. Some considered them possibly the best college team ever (and then the 2020 Alabama team showed up).

What makes a football team great? Some might say, "A great coach." That certainly helps. But without strong players, the coach can do only so much. Another person might argue, "The team needs a star quarterback." Again, that makes a difference. But without a good offensive line, the quarterback will never have time to throw effective passes. A third person might insist, "Defense wins games." Yes, a great defense is important. But the team still needs points on the board to walk away with a win.

Every championship team wins differently. Some win with a running game. Others with passing. Some are defensive giants. (While a few are lucky enough just to be in weak divisions.) But regardless of the strategy, most winning teams have a few common ingredients.

- They have drive and desire.
- They have a strong work ethic.
- They have good chemistry.
- They have a clearly defined strategy.
- They learn to win together.

The same is true in churches. Not every church can achieve *it* the same way. They'd be foolish to try. Not every church has a charismatic preacher or a well-known worship pastor. Not every church can afford a nice building. Not every church can bus in hundreds of kids to their youth ministry or host a large vacation Bible school. Not every church has sermon clips that go viral or has thousands of downloads on YouTube.

Though no two churches achieve *it* the same way, I've found that churches that have it share certain qualities. As I said in the last chapter, as we studied our campuses and looked at churches around the world, our leaders asked questions.

- What contributes to *it?*
- What breathes life into it?
- What brings more of it?
- What slows it?
- What hinders it?
- What kills it?

And we discovered the seven It Factors that seem to exist in every ministry that has *it.*

1. Vision
2. Divine focus
3. Unmistakable camaraderie
4. Innovative minds
5. Willingness to fall short
6. Hearts focused outward
7. Kingdom-mindedness

In part 2, we will look closely at each one. Let's start with vision. I want to help you see it. (Notice what I did there? Bad joke, I know. Please keep reading.)

CHAPTER 4

Vision

The only thing worse than being blind is having sight but no vision.

—Helen Keller

This is a chapter about . . . Hang on just a minute while I check my notes. Uh-oh, I don't have any notes.

Well, I'm pretty sure this is the chapter about . . . uh . . . vision? Yeah, that sounds right. Vision. Our first leadership ingredient is vision.

Now, what can I come up with to say about vision? Besides what my optometrist told me last week. Oh, that reminds me. Gotta get a new plunger for the master bathroom. And flea treatment for the dog.

What? Oh, now where was I? Vision . . .

One, two, three, four . . . eighty-four, eighty-five . . . Wow, ninety-five words already.

Now one hundred. Only 3,900 to go on this chapter. That shouldn't be too hard. Just keep typing, Craig.

Hmm. Let's see, what do I want to say next? I sure hope this chapter ends up somewhere good.

Did You Get It?

Are you still reading?

I hope so, because I was joking, attempting to illustrate a point. Trying to write a chapter with no direction—with no vision for its purpose—would be disastrous. It would be a huge waste of time for both of us.

But as silly as it sounds to write a chapter with no vision, think how foolish it would be to lead a church without vision.

It happens way more often than you might think.

The title of my first book, *Chazown,* is a Hebrew word that means "a dream, a revelation, or a vision." You can find the word thirty-four times in the Old Testament. Proverbs 29:18 is the best-known verse containing *chazown.*

Look at how the Hebrew term in this verse is translated into English in some popular versions of the Bible:

- "Where there is no *revelation,* people cast off restraint" (NIV).
- "Where there is no *vision,* the people perish" (KJV).
- "When people do not accept *divine guidance,* they run wild" (NLT).
- "Without *prophetic vision* people run wild" (GW).
- "Where there is no *prophecy,* the people cast off restraint" (NRSV).
- "If people can't *see what God is doing,* they stumble all over themselves" (MSG).

No matter how you translate it, without *chazown* (vision, revelation, divine guidance), the people we lead will be confused, scattered, unfocused, and easily distracted. Without a God-given vision, our ministries will never get *it* or keep it. Unfortunately, this is how many ministries and organizations function: visionless and without *it*.

Think of it this way: Have you ever driven a car with the wheels out of alignment? If so, you know what happens. Even though you try to keep the car in the middle of the road, it pulls to one side. It's a constant struggle to keep traveling in the intended direction. Over time, misalignment causes major problems. The tires wear out. And much worse, the poorly aimed wheels could pull you off the road into a crash.

Without a God-given vision, our ministries will never get *it* or keep it.

People in a visionless church are like that. Without a compelling vision, the people are busy doing *something*. They're going along doing church, but they are easily pulled off center. They're moving with no destination in common.

Without an alignment of vision, people, just like tires, quickly wear themselves out. Those who serve often burn out. Staff members grow frustrated. Boards, elders, deacons, and leaders often disagree. (Have you ever witnessed a good old-fashioned deacon fight? It makes a Fast and Furious movie seem slow and not so furious.) The ministry may have tons of activity, but there's little spiritual movement. And just like cars, when misaligned, ministries can crash.

Keep Chasing *It*

Ministries that have *it* always have a clear vision. The people know, understand, believe, and live out the vision. The vision guides, motivates, energizes, and compels them. Large numbers of people passionately move in the same direction.

Ministries with vision tend to have *it*.

The rest? Not so much.

It's a little like greyhound dog racing, a popular gambling sport.

To keep the greyhounds running in the right direction, a man in the press box controls a mechanical rabbit, keeping it just in front of those dogs so they never quite catch it. The dogs chase the fake rabbit all the way around the track. True story: One time at a track in Florida, the man in the press box got ready to start the mechanical rabbit. All of the dogs were crouched in their cages. When he pushed the start button, the rabbit took off and the dogs chased. But as the rabbit made the first turn, a short in the electrical system caused it to explode.

Suddenly the dogs didn't know what to do. There was no rabbit to chase, just a little piece of toasted fur hanging on a wire. With the rabbit gone, some of the bewildered dogs plopped down on the track with their tongues hanging out. A couple of them tried to run through a fence and broke some ribs. The rest of the dogs just sat on the track and howled at the people in the stands. And not one dog finished the race.

Do you have teenagers in your student ministry who act like that? Or adults who serve on some church committee? Do you have anyone who is just plopped down in a pew with their tongue hanging out? Do you know someone causing damage by running off in their own direction? Do you have some church members who are howling at other people, creating problems by what they say, how they say it, what they disagree with? If so, maybe it's because they don't have a mechanical rabbit to chase. Without vision, people perish. Without direction, people drift. Without a goal, motivation wanes. Without a mission, ministries fade. Youth groups lose their life. Once-vibrant churches slowly die. We need a clear and compelling vision that is constantly and enthusiastically communicated.

Habakkuk 2:2 says, "And the Lord answered me and said, Write the vision and engrave it so plainly upon tablets that everyone who passes may [be able to] read [it easily and quickly] as he hastens by" (AMPC). Other translations say this vision is supposed to be carried by a "runner" or a "herald," and it should be so clear, displayed so prominently, that people can see it and read it at a glance.

Vision matters. With vision, you have clarity, focus, and direction. A white-hot vision inspires generosity, motivates selflessness, and releases an unstoppable passion to honor God and serve people. Vision empowers a church to have *it*.

On the other hand, without vision, a church or ministry can never expect to have *it*. Without a compelling vision, the organization is quickly pulled off center. People get confused, distracted, and bored. Without even noticing, the mission fades from view as the organization drifts.

Years ago, I took the whole Groeschel crew to a family reunion at the beach. After driving seventeen hours crammed in a minivan with a bunch of kids screaming "I've gotta go" and "Are we there yet?" we finally saw water, waves, and sand. *Hallelujah!* Moments after unpacking the luggage, my kids and I dashed for the water. We were body surfing, floating on our backs, and singing the *Jaws* theme while pointing and screaming, "Shark!" (Other families didn't appreciate it much.)

After a long time of swimming, floating, and playing in the ocean, I looked toward shore for our beach lodging. *It was gone!* Vanished. Our rented beach house was no longer there.

No, I wasn't smoking something illegal. Finally, I realized the house had moved way down the beach. Well, *we* had moved. Without even noticing it, we had drifted. Slowly but surely the gentle current carried us away from our starting point. The current wasn't strong enough to get our attention, but over time, the result was impossible to miss. We had drifted faster and farther than we might have expected.

That's what happens to churches. Without a consistent and compelling vision—constant orientation by fixed landmarks—they drift.

Keep the Vision Current

A ministry with a God-given and passionately communicated vision typically gets *it*. But just because they have it doesn't mean they'll keep it. Old vision is a lot like popcorn left out on the counter for several days. Have you ever tasted stale popcorn? The only thing worse is stale vision. If a ministry loses its vision (or even fulfills its old vision), it's only a matter of time before it loses what made it special in the first place. Without vision, the people quickly lose *it*.

In my hometown, I watched a church that had a burning vision to pay off their financial debt. The whole church rallied around this vision to become debt free. I'd never thought that a church could explode with growth around a debt-reduction campaign, but this one did. During this season of ministry, they had *it*.

Their goal was clear. Ministries aligned. Faith grew. New people started getting saved and baptized. Several hundred new people joined the church. They went from one service to two. The members gave sacrificially and enthusiastically. People were pumped. This church had a compelling vision, a big goal in mind, and they attacked the goal passionately.

They had *it*.

Several years later, this church successfully paid off several million dollars' worth of debt. Vision accomplished. Most would assume that *now* they were positioned to explode with growth. With all of the additional resources available to them, surely the ministry would soar like never before. Certainly, they'd continue to reach even more people, change even more lives, and make an even bigger difference.

The opposite happened.

No one had given much thought to what they would do once they successfully paid off all their debt. Now with more resources than ever, the leadership wondered what to do next. *Should we build a new building? Start a new campus? Hire more staff? Maybe we should give money away. Or perhaps we should put some in the bank for a rainy day.*

So many options.

So little vision.

Finally, after a year of stumbling around trying to find something to get excited about, the church initiated a building project. Midway through (believe it or not), they changed their plans, deciding to put the project on hold to start a different one.

Some people who had given money for the first project were confused, hurt, even angry. A few left the church. Within two short years, the church drifted from health and vibrance to struggle and stagnancy. The people didn't know what to do, what to get excited about, what to give their lives to. Still more people left. This church that had grown around a vision started to die without one. When they had a vision, they had *it*. When they lost their vision, they lost it.

Define Your Vision

Do you have a vision? Many churches and organizations have a vision statement. But in reality, they have no vision. Just because you have words on a banner, website, or business card doesn't mean your leadership has a God-given vision. An idea is not a vision. Maybe you have an idea, but is it a

An idea is not a vision.

God-inspired idea? There's a huge difference between a good idea and a God idea.

Without a vision, people become comfortable with the status quo. Later, they grow to love the status quo. Eventually, they'll give their best to protect what *is*, never dreaming about what could or should be.

They need a vision with definition.

What are some of the problems of a visionless ministry? When there is no vision:

- Most ideas seem like good ideas. This leads to overprogramming and burnout.
- There is nothing compelling to give to. This leads to a consumer mindset instead of a contributor mindset.
- Organizations focus inward. This leads to a slow and painful death.
- Instead of working together toward a common goal, people compete for resources.

Many churches today are visionless. They've drifted. If you ask most church leaders, "What's your ministry about?" they'll give you a predictable response:

- "We're about loving God and loving people."
- "We're about reaching up and reaching out."
- "We're about preaching God's truth to set people free."
- "We're about teaching eternal truths in contemporary ways."
- "We exist to know Jesus and make him known."

If you look at what the ministry is doing and measure it against its claims, what you find is often inconsistent.

Here's a way to look at it: If a martian came to visit earth . . . (Work with me, okay?) Let's say his name is Chad and that he is a CSI martian who has come to investigate your church. (Still with me?) Alien Chad examines your church. What would he conclude you're about?

Chad might think some churches are an entertainment business: people come, watch the show, clap if it's good, laugh when it's funny, cheer when it's exciting, put their money in a bucket, then leave.

He might think some churches are self-help facilities: find out how to fix your marriage, raise your kids, manage your money, get rid of stress, stop your addictions, and make good decisions.

And he might think that some churches are country clubs: dress in your best clothes, greet and be greeted, see and be seen, enjoy the fellowship, pay your dues, and enjoy all the benefits of membership.

Obviously, these examples are extreme. But if Chad the CSI martian knew nothing about your vision and observed everything you do all week long, what would he think? Would Chad say, "That church is all about someone named Jesus"?

Finding the Vision

Years ago, I was part of a ministry at a church that formed a committee of forty people who were determined to discover the church's five-year vision. This brave group of laypeople interviewed dozens of church members. Everyone shared their great ideas. After months of listening, dreaming, and planning, guess what happened? The vision became "Let's do everything."

I'm not joking. This midsized church decided to do just about every good thing you could ever think of—and more. The committee decided to have car-care ministry, busing ministry, elderly ministry, homeless ministry, single adults ministry, Sunday school ministry, Wednesday night Bible study, small groups ministry, shut-ins ministry, quilting ministry, ministry to business professionals, music lessons ministry, handbell-choir outreach ministry, a day care, daily devotions, a radio ministry, a choir internship, a reading club ministry, and a floss-the-teeth-of-elderly-shut-ins ministry. (Okay, I made up that last one. But all the rest were real, and I could add more to the list.)

Hopefully, the *leaders* of your church will seek God, find a divine burden, examine their resources and context, and present a Spirit-breathed, God-sized vision. Notice that I italicized the word *leaders*. If you're the leader of a ministry, this is your role. That certainly doesn't mean you won't listen to people, seeking their wisdom and input. But ultimately, the vision comes from the leader's time of hearing from God.

You might be thinking, *This section is not for me because I'm not in leadership.* While you might not have a formal leadership role, you can still lead. At its core, what is leadership? Leadership is influence. The good news is, you have influence. Whether or not you have a title, your role, gifts, and contribution always matter in God's church.

Here are a few questions to stir your vision. (You might want to jot down some answers. Or maybe your team could explore these questions together.)

1. Why does your organization exist? (If you can't answer this clearly, I'll bet you an overpriced latte there are a few things your organization should stop doing immediately.)
2. What can your organization be the best in the world at? (Borrowing from Jim Collins's classic book *Good to Great*.)
3. If you could do only one thing, what would it be?
4. If you left your organization tomorrow, what would you hope would continue forever?
5. Is there an unmet need in your community that your church might be uniquely able to meet?
6. What breaks your heart, keeps you awake at night, wrecks you?

Envision It

As God gives you clarity, you'll want to work hard to communicate this vision. Leadership expert Sam Chand always says, "An effective vision will always be memorable, portable, and motivational."

A great vision statement is *memorable*. If people can't remember your vision, your church will never have *it*.

Have you ever seen a mission statement like this? "We exist to reach as many people as possible in our city for Jesus Christ before

A great vision statement is *memorable*. Your vision must also be *portable*.

he returns for his bride, the church, by loving them, accepting them, teaching them God's uncompromised Word, and empowering them through Spirit-filled discipleship to become fully devoted Christ followers, reaching up, reaching in, reaching out, and building people to exalt, edify, and equip the saints of God to go into all the world and make disciples of all nations, baptizing them in the name of the Father and the Son and the Holy Spirit, for the glory of our God, who reigns forever and ever, amen."

The only thing memorable about that is if you pass out trying to say it all in one breath. You want a vision statement that's easy to remember. Short is best. Make it crisp. Make it clear. Make it memorable.

Your vision must also be *portable*. People should be able to easily communicate it to others. You'll want everyone on your staff and in the church to be able to give "the vision pitch." Wake any one of them up in the middle of the night and they should be able to describe what your organization is about.

One of the greatest compliments I've received as a leader was from my friend, church and leadership guru Lyle Schaller. When he visited our church, he met with staff members at every level in the organization. I remember him smiling as he said, "Craig, your team is brainwashed." I stared at him, concerned. Lyle laughed and said, "They're brainwashed in the best way possible. Everyone— and I mean everyone!—knows the vision and wants to help fulfill it." Your vision needs mobility. Make sure it's portable.

Not only should the vision be memorable and portable, it should also be *motivational*. If your vision doesn't stir people and move them to action, your vision is too small. Your vision must be something that burns in your heart but is too big for you to do on your own. If you could do it, you wouldn't need God. The vision should capture attention and be irresistibly compelling. It should cause agitation, ambition, ignition, maybe even competition to crush your spiritual enemy.

Churches that are vision driven tend to get *it*. Churches that are vision void don't. Here are some benefits of vision:

- People will give sacrificially for it (both financially and of themselves).
- People will tolerate inconveniences for the greater cause.
- People will share it. You cannot put a price tag on buzz.
- The organization (or ministry) will take on a life of its own.
- Opportunities for distraction will decrease.

You'll want to communicate the vision over and over again. Why? Because as others have said, "vision leaks." You can never underestimate the importance of communicating the vision. I always tell our leaders, "Cast vision more than you think you should. When you feel like you've finally done it enough, double it." When you get tired of hearing yourself say the same things again and again, you are just getting started.

As business writer Patrick Lencioni tells us, you are the CRO: the chief reminding officer. Just when you think you've thoroughly explained the vision, it's time to communicate it again. You cannot overcommunicate what you are about. Tell stories about the vision. Illustrate the vision. Reward those who live the vision. Highlight the vision anywhere you see it. Once you've done all of these things, do them all again.

Here are a few of the things we do to communicate the vision:

- We produce simple videos and email them to members and attenders to renew the vision of the church.
- We share video testimonies with the church to celebrate how the vision is changing lives.

- We highlight the vision on social media.
- We preach two series a year that help renew passion for the vision.
- When ministry attempts don't work well, we use failure as a real-time illustration of how we can better fulfill the vision.
- We gather all of the volunteers for times of renewing and celebrating the vision.
- We hold online vision-casting meetings for leaders and volunteers.
- Every January, we invite each attender to invest their lives in the vision.

Ministries that have *it* have a big vision that bears constant repetition.

Three Levels of Vision Buy-In

Ministries that have *it* are filled with people who understand and believe in the vision. Without that, you will have people who might like the ministry but don't understand where it is going.

In my experience, I've discovered three levels of vision buy-in. Ministries without *it* have people at levels 1 and 2. Ministries with *it* tend to have more and more people moving to level 3.

- *Level 1: The people believe in the vision enough to benefit from it.* Like the person who benefits from the service at their favorite restaurant or exercises at the conveniently located gym, these church attenders are people with a constant consumer mind-set. They come to church because they like it. It's easy. It feels good. It's convenient. They receive something from the ministry. To them, that's what is important.
- *Level 2: The people believe in the vision enough to contribute*

comfortably. Like the person who drops some change into a donation jar or participates in a neighborhood watch program, these are people who were consumers but are ready to contribute as long as it's easy. They're happy to help if it doesn't cost much, doesn't take much, and doesn't interfere with their other priorities.

- *Level 3: The people believe in the vision enough to give their lives to it.* These are the people who understand the vision and get it. They recognize their lives are not their own. They belong to Jesus. They exist to serve a cause greater than themselves. They find joy in sacrificial giving and fulfillment in selfless serving. They become part of the lunatic fringe, radically committed to seeking and saving the lost and making disciples of all people. They're willing to do whatever it takes to do what Jesus has asked them to do. They are all in, holding nothing back, bringing their all. They are part of the greatest cause on earth. They don't go to church; they are the church.

Though people may drift toward comfort and complacency, they don't really like it. Deep down, they desire more. Way more. Everyone craves a cause worth fighting for. We want to feel like our lives are significant and have purpose. We love to be part of something bigger than ourselves, something making a real, even an eternal, difference. As leaders, it's our role to seek God, see the vision, communicate it in a compelling way, and invite people to give their lives for the greatest cause on earth—the cause of Christ.

> **Everyone craves a cause worth fighting for.**

See It and Create It

The legendary Walt Disney died before Disney World in Florida was completed. On opening day in 1971, almost five years after Disney's death, someone commented to Mike Vance, creative director of Walt Disney Studios, "Isn't it too bad Walt Disney didn't live to see this?"

"He did see it," Vance replied simply. "That's why it's here."

I love that. It also makes me wonder. What is it that God wants *you* to see so it can become a reality? What's inside you that God wants to draw out to change the lives of others? How does God want to stir the passion and stretch the faith of those in your church to shine the light of Jesus even brighter into this dark world?

Where there is no vision, the people perish. They struggle. They drift. They wander.

Where there is a vision, the people have focus, power, and energy, and lives are changed eternally.

Seek God.

Hear from God.

Receive his vision.

Let it overwhelm you.

Let it consume you.

Let it burden you.

Cast the vision.

Communicate the vision.

Watch the vision spread.

It Factors

- Without vision, the people will never get *it* and keep it.
- Without a compelling vision, staff and volunteers get frustrated, disagree, and burn out.
- *It* doesn't show up on its own. It follows big vision.
- The vision must be memorable, portable, and motivational.
- You can't overcommunicate vision.
- People give sacrificially toward, tolerate inconveniences for, and love to share a compelling vision.

Questions for Discussion or Reflection

1. Proverbs 29:18 says, "Where there is no vision, the people perish" (KJV). Describe an area of your ministry that is struggling because it lacks vision.

2. Can you pinpoint an area (or areas) in which your ministry has drifted from your vision? What do you need to do to pull it back to the center?

3. Can you clearly define your vision? Why does your ministry exist? Don't skim over these questions. You might want to put the book aside and pray for a while. Make sure you can answer this before you go on: What has God uniquely prepared your ministry to accomplish?

4. There are three levels of vision buy-in. Some believe in the vision enough to benefit from it. Others believe in it enough to contribute comfortably. Ideally, people believe in the vision enough to give their lives to it. What percentage of your staff is at the third level? What about the people in your ministry? What can you do to increase the number of those who will give their lives for God's work?

CHAPTER 5

Divine Focus

Most people have no idea of the giant capacity we
can immediately command when we focus all of our
resources on mastering a single area of our lives.
—Tony Robbins

Our son Stephen was seven when he started to really struggle in school. This surprised us because he had always been a good kid and was exceptionally bright. Whenever he tried to read, he got extremely agitated and started fidgeting. We encouraged Stephen to focus. He seemed to ignore us. We became frustrated.

Finally, we took Stephen to the optometrist. They did all the tests. (I hate that one where they blow a puff of air into your eye. Why?!) It turned out Stephen had weak eyesight. *That's* why he was struggling.

When they put glasses on Stephen, he fell silent. His mouth dropped open. Bless his heart, he half cried and half smiled. The rest of the day he was running around pointing at everything. I never will forget him shouting, "Leaves! Leaves! Look at the beautiful leaves."

It's amazing what vision, what focus, can do.

To get *it,* we need divine focus.

Business consultant Nido Qubein says, "Nothing can add more power to your life than concentrating all your energies on a limited set of targets." The apostle Paul showed his focus when he said, "But *one thing* I do: Forgetting what is behind and straining toward what is ahead, I press on toward the goal to win the prize for which God has called me heavenward in Christ Jesus" (Phil. 3:13–14, emphasis mine).

To get *it,* we need divine focus.

Our second ingredient that leads to *it* is divine focus.

In my observation, ministries that have *it* tend to be focused on a limited set of targets. They do a few things as if all eternity hinged on their results, and they do these things with godly excellence. They clearly see the vision and drive toward it with laser-guided precision. Those who have *it* know what they are called to do. Perhaps just as important (maybe even more so), they also know what they are *not* called to do. Their vision is characterized by specificity. Selectivity. Exclusivity.

To be clear, focused ministries don't necessarily see immediate and overwhelming results. It often takes time, patience, discipline, and endurance. Then one day after weeks, months, or even years of faithfulness and commitment to a focused mission, they wake up and discover that God is doing something special in their midst—they have *it.* Sweet mystery of life, at last I've found you!

These churches are almost obnoxiously passionate about a few important things. They choose to passionately ignore the rest. Their zeal and effectiveness attract the right leaders. The right leaders use their gifts and give their lives to make a difference. And God blesses them with *it*—his mysteriously awesome presence and power.

Unfortunately, when a ministry is faithful and one day wakes up and has *it,* they can be blinded by their success. Instead of seeing with the crystal-clear vision that helped attract *it,* they find their vision becomes clouded. Instead of staying focused on the main thing, the leaders become distracted. The very thing that God blessed—strategic obedience to his specific calling—is one of the first things successful ministries unknowingly abandon. Have you seen that happen? I'm guessing so, because the story is all too common.

The first time I was part of a ministry that had *it* was in college. A few of my party friends and I stumbled into starting a small Bible study. Did I say Bible study? Not quite. About eight or ten of us would gather—before going out drinking—to read a chapter of the Bible and pray that God would protect us as we partied. But God was up to something. One by one, he was drawing us to himself. God quickly and dramatically redirected our lives toward pleasing him instead of ourselves.

Through that small group of students, God lit a spark that spread to hundreds across the college campus, and I was one of the ones who caught fire. Although I was one of the newest believers, I was one of the most excited (and obnoxious) and was thrust into being one of the two leaders of the group. With zero Bible knowledge, zero ministry experience, and nothing more than simple passion for the one who'd just changed my life, I attacked the campus with the love of Christ like I'd never attacked anything in my life. (This was before I met Amy and had her spaghetti. That sauce was the next thing I would attack with such vigor.)

Because we had come to Christ as a result of reading the Bible, our focus was simple. Get people to read the Bible. That was it. Nothing more. Nothing less. Our goal was to get anyone and everyone to gather to read God's Word. No group was ever more naive than we were. If the Bible said it, we believed it was possible.

When the Bible said God would answer our prayers, we prayed—and he answered our prayers. When the Bible said to pray for those who were sick, we prayed—and God often healed the sick. When the Bible said to sell something and give the money to the poor, we did just that. When the Bible said we were the salt and light of the world, we took that direction and told everyone we knew about Jesus.

God gave *it* to our little Bible study. As people all around us read God's Word, they seemed to get *it*. It was one of the most extraordinary works of God I've ever seen.

People were saved. Lots of them. Athletes came to Christ. Professors were baptized. Sorority girls left keg parties to pray. One girl with really bad eyesight was healed. Everyone on this small campus knew something was happening. The word spread, and so did *it*.

This little band of untrained, immature, but sincerely passionate people experienced the kinds of things you read about in the book of Acts. God had given us *it*—his extra dose of real, sincere, Spirit-filled life and power. And it was more special than I can describe.

This ministry grew so quickly and so large the leaders of the college took notice. Since we weren't an official organization and were causing quite a stir, we were politely—well, actually not so politely—asked to meet off campus. There is nothing like a genuine move of God to threaten the traditional religious establishment.

If you asked us what we were about, we would've told you, "All we do is read the Bible and do what it says." That was it. We had divine focus.

Then one day, someone had a good idea.

Notice I said a good idea, not a *God* idea. The idea sounded logical. It made sense. It seemed like a natural step in a growing ministry. Little did we know this one small suggestion was the beginning of our losing what had helped bring *it*—divine focus. Someone once said, "If you chase two rabbits, both will escape." As we chased a new rabbit, we had no idea it would subtly lure us away from the heart of our ministry. It was the beginning of our losing focus on what we were about, and the first step we took toward losing *it*.

What was the idea? It wasn't something weird, strange, or inherently dangerous. No one brought a bag of poisonous snakes to handle. No one started leading voodoo chants or drinking poisoned Kool-Aid. No one decided we should all intermarry, build a rocket ship, fly to another planet, and start a new and supernaturally charged race of people.

The idea was a bake sale. To raise money.

That was it. Well-meaning Christians have been doing it since the invention of the oven. Bake something. Find a table. Write prices on poster board. Sit there all day. Raise $34.50 selling goodies to anyone who'll buy them. Ruin the day of people with gluten allergies. It seemed like there was nothing dangerous about our doing a bake sale. It was so small. It just wasn't at the core of who God had called us to be.

As I reflect, I'm not sure why we thought we needed money. We didn't have any expenses. We didn't even take an offering every week. Money wasn't even on our radar. But other ministries raised money, so why not?

That was the beginning of the blur.

We baked goodies. We sold goodies. We raised some cash. For the first time ever, we had money to spend. Someone suggested we use it to take a few people on a weekend planning retreat. We'd brainstorm. We'd plan. We'd dream up some ways to make the ministry really special (ignoring that it was already special). Sounded like a good plan. So we took an overnight trip to plan how we could make our Bible study even better than it was. That's when our vision blurred and we compromised our focus.

On our brainstorming getaway, someone suggested we start taking a weekly offering. Another person recommended we all do a missions trip to Mexico. Someone else proposed that we pay one of the volunteers a small salary because she was working hard and struggled to pay rent and stay in college. Two others thought we should take our ministry to high schools to evangelize. That led to a suggestion that we form a team of traveling speakers. Another was convinced we were supposed to bring in a real pastor from down the street to teach to make it all more official.

Over the next few months, we tried all of those ideas and more. We'd taken our eyes off the target. The one thing God was blessing was helping others know him through his Word. We took attention away from that one thing and added dozens of other things, and wondered why over the next few months we were losing *it*.

Warren Buffett said, "The difference between successful people and really successful people is that really successful people say no to almost everything." Rather than doing lots of things halfway, we choose to focus our energy. Because doing the wrong new things, things that usurp what God calls us to do, is dangerous. Focus tends to let *it* breathe. Lack of focus generally suffocates it.

Too Many, Too Much, Too Bad

In Luke 10, a woman named Martha was overwhelmed with all of the responsibilities of hosting Jesus. While she was doing everything possible, her sister, Mary, simply sat at Jesus' feet. Martha complained to Jesus, asking him to instruct Mary to help her. "'Martha, Martha,' the Lord answered, 'you are worried and upset about many things, but few things are needed—or indeed *only one*. Mary has chosen what is better, and it will not be taken away from her'" (Luke 10:41–42, emphasis mine). What fascinates me is that if any of us were watching the scene, we would have thought Martha was in the right. She had a servant's heart. She was trying to meet every need. What's wrong with that? Isn't that what our churches pride themselves on? Well, apparently, what God is looking for, what God honors, is focus on only one thing.

To have *it*, you have to choose not to do everything. Those who attempt to do everything always lose *it*.

An Italian proverb says, "Often he who does too much does too little." (Smart people, huh? No wonder they're called *Italians*.) Too many ministries are doing too little by doing too much. For example, a lot of pastors boast about how many ministries they have in their church. One time I met a guy with a church of about four hundred people (with a staff of eight) who told me he had 187 different ministries in his church. I didn't know whether he was bragging, asking me to pray for him, or making the case for a frontal lobotomy.

> To have *it*, you have to choose not to do everything.

I could hardly get my mind around what he said. *One hundred and eighty-seven ministries!* Trying hard not to reveal my shock, I asked which ones were the most important and effective. Smiling sincerely, he said, "All of them." Then he said they hoped to start many more. As the old country preacher used to say, "The devil doesn't have to make you bad if he can just make you busy."

That pastor's church is smaller this year than it was last year, and last year it was smaller than the year before. To me, this doesn't sound like a focused vision. It sounds like ministry schizophrenia. (The voices are telling me to start a new ministry . . . I must start a new ministry.)

Jim Collins in his book *Good to Great* referenced the ancient Greek parable of "The Fox and the Hedgehog." Day after day, the cunning fox plans his attack on the unsuspecting hedgehog. But no matter how creative the fox is, the hedgehog always wins. Why? The fox knows many things, but the hedgehog knows one essential thing. Each time the fox attacks, the hedgehog simply rolls up into a ball of sharp spikes, creating an impenetrable defense. It's what he does best.

That brings us back to Collins's question, which we encountered in the last chapter: What can you be the best in the world at? In ministry terms, what do you do best? If you could do only one thing in ministry to make the biggest impact, what would you do? Think about that. Wrestle with the question. Allow it to consume your thoughts. Read the question again and don't move on until you can answer it with confidence: If you could do only one thing in ministry, what would you do?

The To-Don't List

If you *aren't* interested in having *it,* just start a bunch of random ministries. The more a church does, the less likely they are to have *it.* Why? Because it's impossible to have 187 *effective* ministries in one church. It's challenging even to have only three effective ministries.

Many great businesses understand this principle. One example is In-N-Out Burger. Not only do they have cultlike fans, but the chain is also very profitable. They offer only a few items. When I wrote this book in 2008, I pulled up their website and it read, "Ordering as easy as 1, 2, 3." They offered me three choices:

1. The Double-Double with fries and a drink
2. The Cheeseburger with fries and a drink
3. The Hamburger with fries and a drink

Now almost a decade and a half later, most people would guess they would have expanded their options, right? Well, I just pulled up their website. Guess what you can get? The Double-Double. The Cheeseburger. The Hamburger. French fries. Your choice of beverages. Yep, that's it. Well, almost it. They do have a link to click called the Not So Secret Menu. See, I knew they'd expand what they offered! Wrong again. They don't offer more items (as the urban legend says), they are just willing to customize the few things they offer. They have kept to their limited menu. That's focus.

In-N-Out Burger knows burgers, fries, and drinks (especially shakes, if you ask for my opinion). Notice they're not selling waffles, lattes, or taco salads with guacamole. They're not offering 187 different kinds of burgers. They are offering just three. They're a hedgehog. (Fortunately, they don't make their burgers out of hedgehog.)

Instead of thinking about what you want to add to your ministry to-do list, maybe you should pray about what to add to your ministry to-*don't* list. Some call it planned abandonment. You are planning what things you won't do, which most do, to do best what God has called you to do. (Did that make sense? If not, read it again slowly.) To be great at a few things and experience *it,* you have to say no to many things.

As Steve Jobs famously said, "People think focus means saying yes to the thing you've got to focus on. But that's not what it means at all. It means saying no to the hundred other good ideas that there are. You have to pick carefully. I'm actually as proud of the things we haven't done as the things I have done. Innovation is saying no to 1,000 things."

This sounds counterintuitive. Most people think you do more by doing more. Read that back. You do more by doing more. It reads like a truism, but it's not true at all. You do more by doing less—and doing it well. If you say yes to many different things, you lose focus and effectiveness. That's why you ruthlessly must say no. You don't grow with your yeses. You grow with your nos.

You grow with your nos.

You might need a conjunction change.

Do you remember the song "Conjunction Junction" from *Schoolhouse Rock*? (It was the one that played right before "I'm Just a Bill." Sorry to date myself like that.) Maybe you need a conjunction change that could drastically improve your ministry. Most people say "and" much of the time. We need to say "or" most of the time. For example, instead of saying, "We can do a singles ministry and a counseling ministry and a sports ministry and missions and divorce care and a puppet ministry and a knitting ministry and a ministry for people being stalked by their imaginary girlfriends," we need to say, "We can do this or that and do it well. We can't do it all. Let's focus on what God is calling us to do."

Cutting Back to Move Forward

In the last chapter, we talked about the importance of vision. Don't let your vision become blurry. Busyness blurs ministry vision. Instead of planting more ministries under your direct care, maybe you need to consider pruning the ministry vine.

Thom Rainer and Eric Geiger, in their book *Simple Church,* define focus as "the commitment to abandon everything that falls outside of the simple ministry process."[1] Following their definition, ask yourself, what are we doing that doesn't directly contribute to our vision in a high-impact way? Think about it. Be honest. Let me ask you the question again. This is too important to miss. What are you doing that isn't directly contributing with high impact to your vision? The answer to that question needs to be eliminated.

Gasp.

I can feel you shudder. Your blood pressure is rising. You might be thinking, *If I kill that ministry, what will people do?*

You're imagining the gossip.

You see people getting mad and leaving the church.

You're reading the negative comments about you on social media.

You visualize yourself delivering pizza for a living.

I acknowledge that cutting a ministry can be traumatic. But as with any lifesaving surgery, it nevertheless needs to be done.

For example, we created what we hoped to be our third significant app around the Bible. (Can you see the common thread back to my college days?) Our first was the YouVersion Bible App. Our second was the Bible App for Kids. The third app, which we just knew would revolutionize social media and the Bible, was called Bible Lens.

With unbridled excitement, our developers created an app that could recognize almost any object in any photo you took with your phone. Once you snapped the photo, our custom software would recognize the item in the photo and suggest related Bible verses. Then it would help you artistically display the perfect verse on your photo to post on social media.

If you took a picture of shoes, the app might pick a verse about walking with God. If you took a picture of the sky, you would have your choice of verses about heaven. If you took a picture of your bologna sandwich, you could add to it a verse about Jesus' being the bread of life. Brilliant, right? Yeah! Only it wasn't widely used.

We still think our breakthrough idea was brilliant. Many of the best developers still stand in awe of how the technology works. But because it was only marginally successful, we shut down the app. Some people were hurt, others angry. But since it didn't hit our desired focus on Bible engagement, we cut it to shift resources to something that makes an impact.

You may have to cut a ministry, or you might simply take a break from an activity. I remember having a conversation with my friend Pastor Rick Warren. For years and years, Saddleback Church has impacted thousands of leaders through Purpose Driven conferences. After praying faithfully, Rick and his team decided not to do conferences for a while. Instead, they chose to gather smaller groups and have conversations. Rick devoted several years to interacting with other leaders rather than teaching them.

I heard about one church that suspended all of its ministries (except weekend worship) for the summer. At the end of the summer, they restarted only the few that they believed contributed to the vision.

Pruning Our Ministry Vine

Let me tell you part of our church's story to illustrate. We grew slowly in the early days. For the first few years, I never felt like we were a real church. In my warped mind, I believed we needed our own building and all the other things real churches have—like a sports ministry, concerts, conferences, and our own church van. I thought those important elements would give us *it*. Then we'd be a real church.

Little did I realize, we already had *it*. God was doing something special. Lost people were being found. Found people were growing. The church was spiritually vibrant. All without any of the things I thought were necessary.

One day we built the building I'd dreamed about. A little later, we started the sports ministry that I just knew was necessary. Before long we held a real concert with tickets and overpriced, low-quality T-shirts for sale. Then we hosted a marriage conference featuring a well-known speaker who had his own radio show. Eventually, we even bought our very own van so our students could play Truth or Dare in the back and dare each other to French-kiss while traveling home from camp. (At least that's what I used to do.)

We had arrived! Legitimacy at last.

Then one day I realized that everything I'd always wanted was slowly killing everything I already had. Our church had *it* and we didn't know it. That led us to add things we didn't need, which strangled what we already had. All the new things we finally started doing didn't contribute to the vision. They competed with the vision. We were directing tons of resources into nonproductive areas.

> One day I realized that everything I'd always wanted was slowly killing everything I already had.

Finally, I recognized the insanity of it all. I looked at the sports ministry and realized that we were taking Christians out of their work leagues with non-Christians so they could play together with Christians (but act like non-Christians). How stupid was that?

Our concerts cost us a ton of money and even more time and effort basically to entertain Christians who went to other churches. Stupid again.

Another time we spent a small fortune to bring in one of the best marriage-conference guys, but only eight couples showed up. Stupid on steroids.

Then one of the tires on our van blew out on the highway, rolling the van and throwing several people out onto the side of the road. (No one was killed or permanently injured. Praise God for his protection.)

That's when I decided we didn't need the sports ministry, concerts, conferences, or church van. Without them, we could still be a real church. After more time in prayer, our leaders decided to cut all but five ministry activities. That's right, five. Only five.

What were the five things we did? We focused all of our energy on:

1. Weekend experiences
2. Missions
3. Small groups
4. Kids
5. Students

That's it.

But what about Sunday school? What about Wednesday night Bible study? Vacation Bible school?

Our answer: no.

What about singles ministry? Men's ministry? Women's ministry?

No again.

What about church conferences? Apologetics conferences? Financial management conferences?

Again . . . no.

Christmas pageants? Easter productions? Children's musicals?
Absolutely not.

To some of you, I just became a heretic. Others might think I'm
a hero with superpowers.

For close to a decade, we did only five things. Why? Because we
believed those were the five things God called us and equipped us to
do. Just because you *can* do something doesn't mean you should do it.

At one point we realized we had to loosen our grip, but just a
little. Why?

We recognized that in our early years, when we were smaller,
a few of the things we did outside of our essential five helped us to
grow. They were no longer necessary when we grew larger and thus
didn't make the cut when we narrowed our ministry focus to five.

The issue was when we started launching campuses around the
United States. The campuses typically started small, but because they
were living by our internally initiated focus, they were not able to do
some of the things we were able to do in our early years. Our strict rules
were robbing some smaller, startup church campuses from enjoying
the same opportunities that provided growth for us in our early years.

So we softened our stance. But not much. We allow our smaller
campuses to do occasional neighborhood outreaches. But even after
giving a bit of flexibility, we are still biased to guard our focus with
lots of nos.

I encourage you to do the same.

No matter what, the vision stays central.

Think Priorities

When you narrow your focus, I encourage you not only to think
programs but also to think priorities. I'll explain. I meet for training
with our campus pastors three times a year. During one training

session, I asked them to list on a notecard the top five priorities that would contribute to reaching new people and growing the church. I read their lists aloud. They had lots of good themes, including developing the staff, investing in and appreciating volunteers, caring for church members, stewarding resources, creating an evangelistic atmosphere, and leading the weekend services with excellence. All of their ideas were solid and helpful. But they forgot one thing. And the one thing they forgot was massive.

It sounds offensively simple, but in order to grow and reach more people at church, you must have empty seats. When an auditorium is 80 percent or more full, people don't feel like there is room for them. Most of our church locations have five, six, seven, eight, or even nine weekend services. The problem is that they are almost all full at the two prime times on Sunday. What I know about those who are new to church is that they usually come to one of the two Sunday morning services that are most convenient. Those are the services that are usually way past full.

To grow, we must have room to grow. To me, that's a top priority. But it wasn't listed a single time by any campus pastor. (That wasn't their fault. It was mine.) They had lots of good ideas, but they failed to focus on the one area that would make room for new people to find life in Christ.

When you think focus, don't just think programming. Think priorities. (And if you ask one of our campus pastors today for their number one priority, I promise it won't be developing staff or appreciating volunteers!)

A Great Work

When Nehemiah was faithfully rebuilding the broken walls of Jerusalem, two of his enemies, Sanballat and Geshem, invited him to a meeting with the intention of thwarting his progress. We need to commit Nehemiah's response to memory. The New Living Translation words it this way: "So I replied by sending this message to them: 'I am engaged in a *great work,* so I can't come. Why should I stop working to come and meet with you?'" (Neh. 6:3, emphasis mine).

Nehemiah had *it.* The people with him had *it.* (Can you imagine the thrill of working with people you love, serving the God of heaven, and making history? In the next chapter, we'll examine how this type of camaraderie contributes to *it.*) The people worked together, empowered by God and great leadership, and they accomplished the impossible.

Those who have *it* stick with what brings it. When you know you're doing a great work, do your best not to get distracted. If you have it, guard it. Don't distort it by doing the wrong things. When you increase your focus, you decrease your options. Good things are not necessarily God things. Remember, you grow with your nos.

Tell yourself, "I'm focused. I am doing a great work and I cannot come down."

It Factors

- Those who do it all tend to lose *it.*
- The clearer your vision becomes, the easier it is to guard what God calls you to do.
- Instead of saying "and," maybe you need to say "or."
- If you chase two rabbits, both will escape.
- To be great at a few things and experience *it,* you have to say no to many things.
- Innovation requires saying no to a thousand things.
- When focus increases, options decrease.
- Those who have *it* stick with what brings it.
- You grow with your nos.

Questions for Discussion or Reflection

1. Jim Collins writes about the "hedgehog principle." Look carefully at the people God has put around you, the resources you have available to you, and the people who are within reach of your ministry and answer this question: What can we be the best in the world at?

2. Good can be the enemy of the great. As you narrow in on what you are great at, what good things on your to-do list need to be switched to your to-don't list?

3. Most churches add and add and add ministries. Maybe it's time to prune the vine. If you had to remove one part of your ministry today, what would it be?

4. What few ministries are necessary to fulfill your vision? If you could do only a few things for the greatest ministry return, what things would you do?

CHAPTER 6

Unmistakable Camaraderie

*It is better to have one person working with you than
three people working for you.*
—Dwight D. Eisenhower

We started Life.Church in 1996, the year the movie *Jerry
Maguire* was released. The title character, played by Tom
Cruise, managed the careers of professional athletes. Toward the
end of the movie, after one of those rare emotional guy moments,
Jerry tightly embraced his client and friend Rod Tidwell. Another
athlete observed this with envy and disappointment and asked his
agent, "Why don't we hug like that?" The agent (a money-grabbing
jerk) hesitated, then—you could almost see him thinking, *The things
I do for a buck*—turned and reached for an embrace. The two men
stopped midhug and pulled apart awkwardly.

It wasn't working.

No Faking *It*

Ministries that have *it* enjoy it together. They have the third
ingredient—unmistakable camaraderie. Anyone close to them can

see it. They can feel it. Affinity, community, sincerity, fraternity (and sorority). Christianity at its best. The people love being together. And when they are, when the people interact, it is electric.

Ministries that have *it* enjoy it together. For the church to have *it*, the staff (or volunteers) will likely have it first. As it goes with the leaders, so it goes with the whole organization.

While I'd love to devote time to talking about community in the whole church family, I'll limit the discussion to the staff and volunteers. This is what I'll refer to as "the team."

To have *it* everywhere, it has to start somewhere. It must begin with your team.

Friendships matter. Studies reveal just how important friendships at work are to *it*. "Gallup research shows that close friendships at work boost employee satisfaction by almost 50 percent."[2] Tom Rath, global practice leader at Gallup, explains why employees who have a best friend at work are seven times more likely to be emotionally engaged on the job. He says, "People with friends at work are 96 percent more likely to be extremely satisfied with their life." Happier people make better team members. Yet he reports that fewer than one in five people consider their boss to be a close friend. But when a team member is close to the boss, she is two and a half times more likely to be satisfied on the job.

On our staff, our longest-tenured members are my closest friends. Brian Bruss started when our church was five months old and he had barely reached puberty. (Just kidding, Brian. I know you had already reached puberty. I meant to say you *acted* like you had barely reached puberty.) My assistant and office team leader, Lori Meek, has been part of our church family since 2000. Her team, Adrianne Manning and Stephanie Pok, are like family. Mark Dawson is behind the camera. He's one of the closest friends I have. (And I can never betray him because he can make my nose look bigger on-screen than it already is.)

Bobby Gruenewald, Jerry Hurley, and Sam Roberts are the directional leaders at our church. It's hard for most people to believe, but our directional leadership team (some would call them executive leaders) have been serving together for almost a quarter of a century. Yes, that is extraordinarily rare. And yes, we know what we have is extraordinarily special. When we get together, we laugh so hard we cry. No one is ever safe from being ganged up on. We all love it. All of these team members would tell you that a big part of their ministry satisfaction are the unforgettable memories we share (many of which we won't ever tell a soul).

The team with *it* loves each other. Not only do they minister together, they do life together. What they have is more than friendship. It's something that God gives—more of a partnership of people with deep love committed to a single mission. You're more than friends. You're a team.

Have you heard of the book *Refrigerator Rights*? In it, authors Will Miller and Glenn Sparks talk about how few people today have these rights in each other's lives.

You're probably wondering, *What are refrigerator rights?* Someone with refrigerator rights is a person who feels so comfortable, and is so trusted, they can walk into your home, open your refrigerator, and help themselves to a sandwich and a drink. They don't have to ask.

If you're like most, I suspect very few people have refrigerator rights in your home. Typically, everyone is too busy to really get to know each other. People may have friends at work or the gym or PTA meetings, but few do life together in their homes.

By contrast, teams with *it* are so connected and committed to each other, they almost always have refrigerator rights. When someone else sees *it,* they look on with envy. *Why don't we hug like that? Why can't I open your refrigerator and make myself a bologna sandwich with Dijon mustard and cheese?*

But just as the jerk agent in *Jerry Maguire* couldn't fake a hug, you can't fake this kind of bond. Not every ministry team has *it*. Most don't. And its absence is as obvious as its presence in a team. Instead of humming with a relational buzz, a room of it-less people is mostly silent. When they do talk, it's all business. Little laughter, little joy, little life. They work together, but they don't share *it* together.

What's the Problem?

Why do we find it so difficult to experience the kind of community God created us for and that makes *it* happen?

Pollster George Barna conducted an interesting study which revealed that 95 percent of Americans claim to be independent thinkers.[3] For many people, independence is a virtue, a goal. They want to be financially independent—*I don't need to depend on anyone for money*. They want to be professionally independent—*I don't report to anyone*. And they want to be relationally independent—*I don't need anyone or answer to anyone*.

A businesswoman wants to believe she's a self-made woman. Many athletes are more concerned with their performance than with the results of their teams. Even in marriages, people are often more concerned with what they can get than with what they can give.

Not only are we independent, many people today are afraid. With as much relational pain as they endure, especially those who have served in ministry and leadership roles, it's no wonder they're gun shy. Amy and I talk often about our ministry scars. We've lost some of our closest friends to misunderstandings and half-truths. Doing what we believed was the right thing, we've had to fire people we cared about. Some dislike us to this day. Good friends have left the church feeling bitter toward us, or God, or both. People we opened up to betrayed confidences, dragging us through awkward seasons of pain and fear. For a while, we didn't ever want to trust again. Can you relate? It's kind of like that song by Adele. Actually, it's kind of like *every* song by Adele. You've learned that sometimes love lasts, but sometimes it hurts instead, and you're wondering whether you'll ever love again, and you won't let anyone get close enough to hurt you.

Perhaps there was a time when you opened up to someone about your hurt only to have them belittle your pain. Or you trusted someone who ended up betraying you. Or you gave your heart to someone who walked away and rejected you. Unconsciously, you decided you'd make it on your own. You'd be independent, not needing anyone.

I can't tell you how many pastors and church leaders I've talked to who are terrified to open up. They're paralyzed by fear, certain that if they let someone in, they'll get hurt—again. Maybe that's you. After being burned, you won't let anyone get close enough to hurt you. You're independent, but acutely aware that something isn't right. You might have a constant low-grade frustration. Maybe you're plagued by a nagging sense of melancholy. You live in a persistent state of mild depression. You know something is missing, but you can't put your finger on what it is.

As long as you're afraid of intimacy and spiritual partnership, you likely won't experience *it*. To have *it*, you have to share it with each other. Just as there's no I in *team,* there's no *it* in *independence*.

God told Adam that it isn't good to be alone. Solomon said two are better than one. Jesus said that God is present when two or three gather in his name. Those who have *it* experience it best together.

Ephesians 2:19–21 says, "You are citizens along with all of God's holy people. You are members of *God's family*. Together, we are his house, built on the foundation of the apostles and the prophets. And the cornerstone is Christ Jesus himself. We are carefully *joined together* in him, becoming a holy temple for the Lord" (NLT, emphases mine). God wants us to be active members of his family. We are to be joined together. Henry Ford said, "Coming together is a beginning. Keeping it together is progress. Working together is success."

You can't experience *it* alone. We hear a lot about having a "personal" relationship with Jesus, which is important. But when you read Scripture, you see that God is actually calling us to a "shared" relationship with Jesus. God wants you to share *it*. And yet for so many, the goal is to be independent. These well-intentioned people fail to realize that to be independent is to be distinctly non-Christian.

Did you get that? Many people pursue a goal that is opposed to God's plan. God designed you to be *inter*dependent. He wants you depending on him *and* on his people. If you want *it*, you'll experience it best when you live in authentic community with God's people.

> If you want *it*, you'll experience it best when you live in authentic community with God's people.

Blame the AC and the Garage-Door Opener

Where has the intimacy gone? Why are so many people relationally isolated? Why are people today living mostly independently and often alone? Blame it on the air conditioner and the garage-door opener! That's right. Before the air conditioner, people sat outside on their front porches and got to know one another. They sipped cool drinks, played checkers, and chatted for hours, sharing their lives. They had a healthy, laid-back togetherness. Then an evil enemy invaded our homes—the air conditioner enabled people to stay indoors. In the absence of front-porch connections, neighbors started to drift. Relationships withered.

Enter the invention of the garage-door opener. Suddenly we could completely avoid the neighbors. (I told my kids people used to have to get out of their cars to open garage doors. They stared in disbelief.) Many new neighborhoods have no sidewalks, further discouraging interaction. Instead of having deep and lasting friendships with neighbors, many people hardly even know their neighbors' names.

What's more, technology has relieved us of the need to talk face to face. We can text or email instead, avoiding unpleasant topics and saving the time that deep conversations require. We can bank online, buy shoes online, order pizza online, do all of our Christmas shopping online, order our groceries online, and never have to talk to anyone. We might be dependent on technology, but we no longer seem to be dependent on people.

Have you recognized this independent mindset bleeding into the church? Many people want to come to church services anonymously. Staff members want to work independent of the team. Yet the New Testament is peppered with "one another" reminders. While Scripture says to love one another, encourage one another, offer hospitality to one another, be kind to one another, many people are content tolerating one another, if not ignoring one another. My YouVersion Bible search fails to find those one-anothers anywhere in the Scriptures.

Bringing *It* to Your Team

Some ministry teams have *it*. Some don't. The it-free or it-lite might be called a team, but they are really a group of individuals doing their own thing. A typical church might have a group that thinks about kids' ministry and another that focuses on small groups and another that plans for missions. These groups are compartmentalized in nonporous silos. They're most passionate about what they're doing, forgetting how their role should fit into the overall mission of the church. Even if all the players are spiritual stars, the team will never win unless the players work together. As Babe Ruth said, "The way a team plays as a whole determines its success. You may have the greatest bunch of individual stars in the world, but if they don't play together, the club won't be worth a dime."

The apostle Paul used the body as a metaphor in 1 Corinthians 12:12: "Just as a body, though one, has many parts, but all its many parts form one body, so it is with Christ." We each have our role. One person's role is to be the mouthpiece—communicating the vision. Another has the role of the hands—executing the work daily. Another fulfills the role of the feet—carrying the work and ministry outward. Yet another lives out the role of the spleen— okay, I have no idea what a spleen does, and I don't think I want to!

You get the point. The body needs all of the parts functioning together. A mouth or hand or foot or spleen lying on the ground by itself is not just an independent body part, it's pointless. It's gross! Outside of the body, seeking to work on its own, a body part will cease to function. And it's the same in the church. That's why the independent ministry mindset kills *it*. *It* needs others with *it* to flourish.

No Ministry Is an Island

You might be familiar with the inner workings of staff members competing for a limited number of resources. (I'm not talking about *your* church, of course.) A church's ministries quietly, or loudly, compete for budget dollars. They argue over who gets the use of certain rooms at certain times. Ministries compete for permission to hire administrative help. During building projects, each department might fight for their fair share. Team leaders compete for accolades. *Will they mention me at the staff meeting?* People might compete for the ministry leaders' time.

The problem is that when two parties compete, one loses. That's why in ministry, those who have *it* don't compete with one another; they work to *complete* one another. They love the mission so much they're willing to give and take. They're eager to work hard and play hard. They enjoy the battle, together. When they win, they win as a team. When they lose, they learn as a team. Someone once said, "Teamwork is the fuel that allows common people to attain uncommon results."

Let's examine five common elements that contribute to it-producing camaraderie on a team.

1. Understanding the Big Picture

To be a strong team with *it*, every staff member and volunteer must understand the mission of the organization. This is where vision and camaraderie overlap and enhance each other. If a staff member doesn't see how her role ties into the big picture, she will feel like she is just doing a job. She'll feel undervalued, unappreciated, and unimportant. Her purpose must be expressed explicitly, not just assumed. Everyone needs his or her deserved share of the credit.

Imagine assembling a ten-thousand-piece puzzle. (My wife is smiling as she reads this. I feel nauseated. I'm horrible at puzzles.) If your role is to put ten pieces together in the corner, but you have no idea what difference your part makes, you'll quickly grow bored or frustrated. You'll want to know what you're contributing to. What will the completed puzzle look like? It's the leader's role to constantly point to the target, to express over and over how each person's role contributes. The big picture requires constant exposition.

When a person understands and embraces the mission, they'll enjoy and appreciate the camaraderie of sacrificing together. They willingly give up some things they love for something they love even more—reaching people for Christ. Mother Teresa said, "None of us, including me, ever do great things. But we can all do small things, with great love, and together we can do something wonderful." Without regular reminders of why we do what we do, of how our part contributes to something wonderful, a team will lose *it* and simply be a bunch of people doing their own gig.

Our staff once did an exercise we called Because of You. We asked our staff members to encourage each other by expressing how their role contributes to the larger work of God in the church. The conversation started in a touching way. Someone from our finance team told one of the kids' team members, "Because you write such great curriculum, my child is closer to Christ." Another person shared with someone on the facilities team, "Because you oversee the setup of chairs, God touches lives each week during worship." Before long, people were crying gently. One person sobbed as she expressed with heartfelt emotion, "Because of all of your encouragement and prayers, not only did my marriage survive, but we're closer than we ever could have imagined." Don't expect transparency and vulnerability to just happen; create opportunities for your team to bond. And when they can bond over the mission, in a way that helps them to see the big picture—well, that's when you get *it*.

2. Having Fun Together

Those teams that have *it* enjoy it and enjoy each other. They laugh together, often. When I walk into the midst of an it-filled team in our church, I'm always wary of danger. At any moment, a rubber band could blindside me, a water gun could blast me, or someone could jump out from behind a desk and tackle me. I've been tackled on many occasions. Even full-on blitzed. (But you should see the other guys.)

Teams with *it* have nicknames for everyone. (In case you're wondering, I'm Maverick and my video guy is Ice Man. Can you hear the theme song from the movie *Top Gun*?) They celebrate birthdays. They throw parties for "work-aversaries." They play gags on one another. They take trips together. They tell stories about each other and exaggerate more with each telling. They initiate new members of the team. (I could write a whole chapter on the most outrageous initiations, but many of those fall into the "you had to be there and now you can't tell anyone because we are all sworn to secrecy" category.) Those with *it* enjoy it together.

Okay, I know you're wondering, so I'll go ahead and tell you *one* of the initiation stories. A few years ago, Beau Coffron joined our staff to help oversee our social media ministry. Our communications team wanted to welcome him in their creative (and humorously cruel) way. So this incredibly innovative group of four "decorated" his office.

- *Step 1:* They covered his carpet from wall to wall with strips of two-sided tape. The strips were carefully laid out about three inches apart.
- *Step 2:* They filled hundreds of plastic cups with ice and glitter.
- *Step 3:* They secured the cups on top of the strips of tape. (Can you visualize it? Imagine the floor of an entire office covered from wall to wall with hundreds of cups filled with ice and glitter.)
- *Step 4:* They went home for the night and allowed the ice to melt, creating a rainbow of impassable glory.

Beau arrived the next day, opened his office door, and saw the masterpiece. He laughed, appreciating the team's fun gesture. He laughed because he still didn't quite realize what he was seeing. He tried to lift a cup, and the whole line of cups stuck to that tape strip fell, spilling glitter water all over his office. Every cup was connected to dozens more. Beau had just entered the matrix. A wet, sparkly matrix.

I think Beau worked outside for a week. I honestly have no idea how he solved the problem. (I'm kind of surprised he ever reinhabited his office.)

All great teams provide this type of heartfelt, edifying ministry to each other.

You might be thinking you don't have the funds to have fun.

You can't afford extravagant team-building events. No problem. I've found the best kind of fun isn't something you pay for or even plan. Fun is most often a serendipitous byproduct of fulfilling a mission with people you love.

3. Getting Naked Together

You may have read this subhead and thought, *Now, that might be interesting.* Or if you're more the stuffy religious type, you may have thought, *How disgusting.* Either way, it got your attention, didn't it?

Teams without camaraderie tend to cover up. Teams with great camaraderie get relationally naked, as author Patrick Lencioni would call it. Those without *it* can be two faced. Those with *it* are true faced.

There is no substitute for being transparent. The more real we are, the more likely we'll experience *it*. The more we hold back, the less likely we are to have it. Mark Sanborn, bestselling author and authority on leadership, says, "In teamwork, silence isn't golden; it's deadly."

I refer to those I'm close to as my bare-feet buddies. Amy says she loves everything about me from the top of my head to the bottoms of my ankles. Why the bottoms of my ankles? Because Amy says I have ugly feet. If someone knocks on our door and we don't know who it is, she never says, "Craig, quick, get a shirt on." Topless Craig? No problem. What she always screams is, "Craig, quick, put some socks on. We can't let anyone see your feet!"

My intimate friends can see my feet. (If, of course, they can handle it.) They're my bare-feet buddies. What's more, if your team has camaraderie, the women can show up without makeup. The guys don't have to shave. Everyone is free to burp . . . I'll stop there.

You get the picture. We're open with each other. We bring our real selves. If one is hurting, the others know. We're family.

It is late Sunday evening as I'm typing in my office. Some of our closest friends have just left our home. Amy and I have been exhausted from this season of grueling (yet rewarding) ministry. Instead of sucking it up and striving to appear strong, we had our friends over and let it out and revealed our needs. Our close friends listened intently, then prayed for us passionately. We can already feel God lightening the burden.

Too many in ministry don't feel the liberty to show their real selves. Perhaps without realizing it, they're putting on a spiritual show, acting out a part, all the while suffocating, dying a slow and lonely relational death. Can I encourage you to be yourself? It's scary, but the reality is that people would rather follow a leader who is always real than one who is always right. People may be impressed with your strengths, but they'll connect with you when you reveal your weaknesses.

Psychologist Sidney Jourard writes about the benefits of self-disclosure. He describes it as "a function of attraction and trust." We become fond of people who open up to us. He explains, "When people show that they like and trust us enough to share personal information, we begin to like and trust them in return. As an expression of our new feeling, we are likely to disclose something about ourselves, thus strengthening the positive feelings." That's why closed people rarely make friends. Mark it down: The more open your team is, the more likely you'll experience it together. The more closed you are, the more you'll kill it.

Our staff regularly does 360 reviews. This is when team members review each other. The review starts out anonymously to encourage honesty. As the process continues, we get specific with each other to help one another bond and grow. Here are a few things team members have said about me:

- "Craig is a great communicator and a visionary leader."
- "The most impactful aspect of Craig's leadership is his

radically growing love for Jesus. His ability to transfer what God is doing in him is changing us as an organization."

- "Craig's disconnection with the day-to-day operations can be a problem. His strength of delegating can become a weakness when he doesn't know what is going on."
- "Craig needs to be more engaged with staff members outside his office and floor. He would be surprised at what he may not know."

I was blessed and affirmed by the positive statements. And I was shaken that some consider me too disengaged. Imagine if I didn't provide an opportunity to receive this kind of valuable information. I'd coast along assuming everything was on track without realizing that *it* had sprung a leak.

4. Celebrating the Wins

Many ministries have victories. Few celebrate them. A win is when something goes great. We pray. We plan. We perform. And God blesses. But then we miss *it,* because we skip a critical step. We don't party.

Too many wins go by without celebrations.

I love what Andy Stanley does with his team at every staff meeting. They open their meetings with stories of how lives have been changed. They celebrate the victories, large and small. Everyone gets to enjoy what God has done, expressing together an attitude of gratitude.

Earlier today, I received an email from our youth team leader. One of our campuses had an extraordinary event during which God blew our socks off. (I wasn't there at the moment, which was fortunate because my feet . . . well, you know.) The team leader included our whole staff in the email so we could celebrate the win. Later, when I saw him approaching the building, I tackled him and threw him in the mud to celebrate. All day long he bragged about why his shirt was muddy. He was covered in *it* and he loved it—celebrity for a day.

Teams with *it* look for excuses to celebrate. Anniversaries. Completion of significant projects. Ministry launches. Personal victories. Even funny mistakes, flub-ups, or embarrassing moments can be fun to commemorate. This week, our finance team dressed up in eighties apparel to celebrate something. (I don't know what; I was afraid to ask.) Last week, I saw one guy in a chicken costume break dancing to rap music while his team cheered. (Again, I didn't ask.) Our creative team often brings in food to celebrate birthdays and births of babies. I spend a lot of time testing the food just to make sure it's safe to eat. Don't underestimate the value of helping your whole church enjoy the wins. (My family's grocery bill is down $75 a month.)

Oprah Winfrey said, "The more you praise and celebrate your life, the more in life there is to celebrate." Those with *it* celebrate it together.

> Those with *it* celebrate it together.

5. Fighting Hard behind Closed Doors

Teams that have *it* are like family. Part of being family is fighting. That's right. Teams that have *it* know how to mix it up good and still be friends. They maintain their identity as a team, loyal to the end.

Legendary NBA coach Pat Riley summarized loyalty to the team when he said, "Commitment to the team—there is no such thing as in-between. You are either in or out." Those with *it* are in. The opposite is true for the it-less. On the surface, they may look calm. But underneath, you'll often find a storm forming. People are nice and polite outwardly, but inwardly they are full of resentment and bitterness.

Part of having *it* is knowing that as a group we can have it out and still be friends. Any successful organization knows how to work through conflict. Teams without *it* avoid conflict. Teams with *it* understand that conflict is sometimes necessary to have *it*.

When a church has *it*, things move quickly. Change is constant. If you blink, you've missed something. Because of the rapid pace of progress, people can feel left out, uninformed, or unappreciated. Other times, opinionated people have very different ideas on what should happen. Sometimes these differences can be solved easily and quietly. Other times it takes a good old-fashioned fight to work things out.

Those with *it* know how to fight. When I talk about church fights, I don't mean the kind in which a deacon gets mad at the pastor and punches him at the deacons' meeting, then the pastor's wife gets mad at the deacon's wife and crawls over and grabs her hair and claws her face while all the husbands cheer like they're watching UFC. Those are definitely interesting fights, but they are not productive. When I talk about a fight, I'm referring to shutting the doors and fighting fair in private. People with *it* know how to say what's on their minds, get it out in the open, and not walk out of the room until the issue is settled. Once it's resolved, they act publicly as if the fight had never even happened.

This happened to us recently. At about 9:07 a.m. in our directional team leaders' meeting, I snapped at Jerry and told him why I thought his idea wasn't good. (It wasn't, by the way. I'm sticking to my story.) He pounced back telling me he didn't like my tone of voice. I raised my voice even louder telling him that his dumb idea triggered my bad tone and if he had better ideas, I'd have better tones. The fight was on.

Funny thing is, our church had been named by Glassdoor the best place to work in America. Less than two hours later, I was scheduled to interview Jerry about creating a great work culture because he is the leader I give the most credit for our winning the award and, more important, for creating the culture. How is that for awkward? We fight. Then we do a podcast together about great work environments. Only it wasn't awkward at all. As fast as it blew up (and believe me, it blew up), it blew over. It didn't pass because we swept it under the carpet. It passed when Jerry stopped and owned what he did wrong. I did the same. Then we apologized. We forgave each other. And we did one of the better interviews we've had on the podcast. Because we are loyal to each other, we can fight and recover quickly.

Colin Powell said, "When we are debating an issue, loyalty means giving me your honest opinion, whether you think I'll like it or not. Disagreement, at this stage, stimulates me. But once a decision has been made, the debate ends. From that point on, loyalty means executing the decision as if it were your own." Leaders with *it* fight together privately and stand together publicly. The essential word in both settings is *together*.

As I said, I work closely with three other directional leaders in the church. We actually name our fights and laugh about them. There was the Blindside Craig Fight in which I almost fired them all. There was the Naked by the Fire Pit Fight in which they almost fired me. (For the record, there was a fire pit, but no one was naked.) And the one I just told you about with Jerry? That's the Jerry Had a Dumb Idea Fight.

They Had *It* in Jerusalem

As a pastor of a growing church, I've found it's difficult to go anywhere locally without someone being excited to talk to me. A friend suggested that if I'm in a hurry, I can just put my cell phone up to my ear and pretend I'm in the middle of a conversation. One day, while walking through a big-box store, I gave his suggestion a try. I noticed how a few people politely waved, but no one stopped me. My new plan worked brilliantly until, right in the middle of my "conversation," my cell phone rang. Really loudly.

Busted.

Instead of avoiding relationships and striving for independence,

I'm asking God to make me *inter*dependent, like the believers of the early church. Remember when Peter preached in Jerusalem on the day of Pentecost and three thousand people met Christ? These new believers had *it* in a special way. Without Starbucks coffee in the lobby, four-color mailers, or an awesome website to rely on, these believers depended on God's presence and his people. They had *it,* and it spread rapidly. Scripture shows:

- The believers were devoted to God's Word, to spending time together, and to each other (Acts 2:42).
- Because of their commitment, everyone was blown away by what God was doing (Acts 2:43).
- They were so committed to each other that if someone had a need, someone else would sell something and give the money to them. They were so generous that eventually no one had a need (Acts 2:44–45; 4:34).
- They spent time together in their homes. They had refrigerator rights (Acts 2:46).
- God gave them great favor with people, who begged to be a part. Others saw *it* and wanted it. People were being saved every day (Acts 2:47).

Where is that Acts 2 kind of community today? Instead of giving our lives to each other deeply and depending on one another, many are avoiding each other. The guy at the gym with his AirPods, signaling to everyone, "Leave me alone." The person who spends limitless screen-to-screen time with people, but virtually no face-to-face time. (Can you say Zoom life during the COVID-19 quarantine?) People are doing life alone.

In the next chapter, we'll see how camaraderie, partnership, teamwork, and family, fueled by passion from God, can overcome almost any obstacle by contributing to another It Factor—innovative thinking.

It Factors

- People on teams that have *it* enjoy it together.
- As long as you're afraid of intimacy and spiritual partnership, you likely won't experience *it*.
- God is calling us to more than just a personal relationship with Jesus. He wants us to experience a *shared* relationship with him.
- Those who don't have *it* compete with one another. Those with *it* complete one another.
- We need to take time to celebrate our wins together.
- To have *it,* you have to share it with each other. *It* dies when it is alone.
- Leaders with *it* understand the big picture, have fun, get naked, celebrate the wins, and fight behind closed doors.

Questions for Discussion or Reflection

1. Many people are striving for independence rather than learning to be interdependent. How are the people in your ministry growing together and becoming more dependent on God and one another? How are those around you isolating and becoming more independent? What needs to be done to make improvements?
2. Teams that have *it* enjoy it together. They have a blast with each other. How is your organization fostering great team spirit? What are you doing in your everyday interactions that everyone enjoys? What are your plans to develop camaraderie?

3. How well do your team members know one another? Would people describe your organization as a caring environment? How many of your team members have refrigerator rights at your house? What could you do to invite more people into your life and the heart of the team? Do you have a best friend at work? How would your other team members respond to that question?

4. How well do your team members understand the big picture? Do people know the value of their role and see how it fits in the grand scheme? Or do they feel like they're just doing a job? Are your team members competing for resources or completing each other? Explain. What can you do to better paint the vision and show value to those who are serving?

CHAPTER 7

Innovative Minds

Innovation is not absolutely necessary, but then neither is survival.

—Andrew Papageorge

Imagine I asked you, "Could you come up with a hundred thousand dollars in cash by the end of this week?" Chances are unless you're mega rich, you'd probably laugh and say, "Dream on!" I just asked you to do the impossible. You might think, *There's no way I could come up with that kind of cash. I can barely pay my bills.*

Now imagine the people you love most in the world. Your short list might include your spouse, parents, kids, and some close, trusted friends. Think of one of those people specifically. (I'm thinking about my teenage daughter Joy, because she just burst into my room and said, "Daddy, you are the greatest!" She then asked for permission to stay out late with her friends. But I'm still focused on the "greatest" part.) Do you have your person in mind? Good. Let's keep going.

Suppose I told you that your special loved one is very sick. I'm not talking about "I've got to go puke my guts up for an hour, bowing reverently before the porcelain god" sick. I'm referring to "you've got less than a month to live" sick. I'd have your undivided attention.

Now imagine my telling you the doctors are certain your loved one will die this month unless you get them a rare treatment by the end of this week. Because of the scarcity of this treatment, it is *very* expensive.

You're probably thinking, *Money is no object! If this treatment will cure my loved one, I'll do whatever it takes!*

"How much does it cost?" you ask, determined to find the money.

Soberly, I reply, "The shot is one hundred thousand dollars."

What would you do?

Remember a couple of minutes ago you thought finding a hundred thousand dollars in a few days would be impossible. Now your perspective has changed. It will not be easy, but you will find a way to get the money. You might secure a home equity loan. You might call a rich relative. You might sell everything you own. You might create a GoFundMe account. You might even consider knocking off a bank. (I hope not, but you should keep your COVID-19 mask handy just in case.) Why are you willing to go to such extremes? You became motivated.

What changed? In the first scenario, you had no incentive. But the life-or-death stakes in the second scenario made you unstoppable.

The spark of passion ignited the fuel for innovation.

One Idea Could Change Everything

Innovation is different from creativity. Creativity is thinking up new ideas. People with new ideas are not necessarily innovators. People who *do* new ideas are innovators. Author Sarah Ban Breathnach said, "The world needs dreamers and the world needs doers. But above all what the world needs most are dreamers that do." Leaders with *it* do more than just think of new ideas; they actually do the new ideas.

Wikipedia defines innovation as the process of making improvements by introducing something new. If there is any group in the world that should be motivated to make improvements, reflecting God's creative nature, it should be Christians. *Imago Dei* is the Latin term expressing the idea that human beings are created in the image of God. Since we're made in the image of a creative creator, we too should conceive creative ideas. Psychologist, physician, and consultant Edward de Bono said, "There is no doubt that creativity is the most important human resource of all. Without creativity, there would be no progress, and we would be forever repeating the same patterns."

> **Leaders with *it* do more than just think of new ideas; they actually do the new ideas.**

Reflecting God, innovative believers tend to have *it*. This fourth leadership ingredient is borne out of their passion to please God, reach people, and help those in need. That passion drives them to lead like *it* matters. At our church, we often say, "We will do anything short of sin to reach people who don't know Christ. To reach people no one is reaching, we'll have to do things no one is doing." With increasing passion comes increasing creativity to reach people.

The apostle Paul obviously had *it*. And he often did things in new ways. He crossed lines and changed his approach to reach different people. He said, "To the Jews I became like a Jew, to win the Jews. . . . To the weak I became weak, to win the weak. I have become all things to all people so that by all possible means I might save some" (1 Cor. 9:20, 22).

The ministries that have *it* are filled with people so passionate they are driven to innovate. They will become all things to all people or do unusual things to reach those who are far from Christ or to help those who are hurting. Like the four men who broke through the roof to get their crippled friend to Jesus, motivated believers don't see obstacles. They create opportunities.

Instead of saying, "It will never work," they say, "What if this does work?"

Instead of whining, "We can't reach certain people," with faith they exclaim, "We *will* find a way."

While many lament, "We don't have what it takes to make a difference," innovative leaders say, "God is our provider; we have more than enough."

These innovators reflect Robert Schuller's heart when he said, "All it takes is one idea to solve an impossible problem." They commit to find that idea. And they usually succeed.

When *It* Changes

If what your church or ministry is doing now is effective and changing lives, enjoy it while it lasts. Because what's working now won't work in the future. The message we preach must never change, but how we communicate it must change as the world changes. This may sound discouraging, but it's true. If you don't change, you won't last. If you don't adapt how you share the gospel, your effectiveness will likely lessen over time because the world is changing too fast. William Pollard said, "The arrogance of success is to think that what you did yesterday will be sufficient for tomorrow."

If the subject of this book were businesses instead of churches, you'd probably agree with this thought: "The most successful companies of the future will be doing things no one is doing today." If you didn't agree, I'd encourage you to take a walk down memory lane. If you are old enough to remember, think back to 1980. In 1980, Mount Saint Helens erupted, the Rubik's Cube debuted, Post-it Notes became a thing, and I was elected president of my eighth-grade class. (I'm guessing you didn't know about my blowout election. No offense taken.)

If you were into business in 1980, you'd remember some of the biggest companies were General Motors, Walmart, Exxon, and Ford. Fast-forward to today, and the companies in the headlines include Apple, Amazon, Facebook, and Google, all of which did not exist the year I won the big election. It's safe to say they are all doing things that most of us did not even dream possible.

Massive shifts are certainly not limited to business. Let's take churches. The largest churches in America today did not exist in 1980 (or even 1990). Have churches changed? For centuries, when a church gathered, they met in a single building and their ministry was mostly limited to a single community. Then technology and innovation made one church in multiple locations possible. Shortly after, church online became a reality.

If you are ready for change, you are ready for growth. This mindset changes how you see problems. When you think about it, every innovation is really a solution to a problem. Problems aren't things to be feared but opportunities to embrace. Many great innovations are solutions to a problem people did not even know they had. No one was asking for an iPod, iPad, or iPhone. Most people never wanted a device that would listen to you twenty-four hours a day, play music, tell you the weather, and send you whatever you ordered from Amazon. But I use all of those devices today (except the iPod, which is *so* 2002).

If you have a problem in your ministry, think of it as an opportunity. Maybe you have lost a key staff member, you can't find land, or you struggle to stream online. Tell yourself this is not just a problem to solve but an opportunity to seize. Problem equals potential. Because every innovation is a solution to a problem.

Embrace Your Lim*i*tations

In 2006 and 2007, our church was named the most innovative church in America and was featured in *Outreach* magazine. I was honored, yet openly acknowledged that it was the people around me who were the innovative ones. I was just the guy crazy enough to let them try their wacked-out ideas. (For the record, I believe the most innovative leaders are the ones most of us have not heard of yet.)

Because of this honor, I have sometimes been invited to consult and to teach on innovation. Before I speak on the subject, the two most common complaints I hear from leaders are:

1. We just don't have any creative people.
2. If only we had more money, we could be really creative.

While I acknowledge that an abundance of resources opens many possibilities, I suggest these two complaints are simply excuses that prevent many great ideas from becoming reality. Our leaders have stumbled upon something that has changed the way we do ministry. Maybe you've heard the old adage "Where God guides, he always provides." We made up a new saying: "God often guides by what he *doesn't* provide."

Read that again slowly and think about it in relation to your ministry. God often guides by what he doesn't provide. Are you up against a wall with no good plan to get past it? Have you hit an obstacle that appears insurmountable? Maybe God will guide you to see something you wouldn't if he had removed the wall.

A great example of this principle is found in Acts 3. Peter and John were traveling to their afternoon temple prayer meeting when they saw a man who had been crippled his whole life being carried to his begging post. The hurting beggar recognized Peter and held out his cup, hoping to get some change to buy dinner. That's when God started using Peter's limitations—what Peter *didn't* have—to guide him. Think about it. If Peter had had a few bucks on him, it might have been easy to toss a bill toward the man, nod politely, and keep moving to be on time for prayer. But because he did not have what the man wanted, he was able to give the man what he *needed*. Peter said, "Silver or gold *I do not have,* but what I do have I give you. In the name of Jesus Christ of Nazareth, walk" (Acts 3:6, emphasis mine). Then Peter reached down and pulled the man to his feet. I wonder whether this would have happened if Peter hadn't been financially limited.

The truth: you have what you need. Watch out for the excuses. Most of us make them occasionally. Maybe you've thought:

- We could do so much more if our people gave more.
- We could reach more people if we had a better building.
- We could have an awesome ministry if we could afford more staff.

Whenever you're tempted to whine about what you don't have, remember that God has given you everything you need to do everything he wants you to do. Peter wrote, "Everything that goes into a life of pleasing God has been miraculously given to us by getting to know, personally and intimately, the One who invited us to God" (2 Peter 1:3 MSG). If you don't have something you think you need, maybe it's because God wants you to see something you've never seen. Those with *it* recognize that God brings *it*. *It* is not found in the things the eye can see.

God has given you everything you need to do everything he wants you to do.

The truth is, innovation is more about mindset than money. If you believe you can't, you can't. If you believe you can find a way, you probably will. If you think you lack what you need to do what you need to do, you won't do what you need to do even if you have what you need. Having more is not always better. It can be worse. Why? More people can slow things down. More time can make you lazy. More money can train you to buy solutions rather than create them. When you look at the business world, you see this reality. Most innovative companies are startups that don't have much or mature organizations that enforce artificial restraints to push innovation.

The Limitation Can Drive the Innovation

We've raised several critical It Factors of great innovation:

1. *Passion* creates motivation, which leads to innovation. You couldn't come up with a hundred thousand dollars in a few days unless you had a great reason to do it. If there was a reason, you'd find a way.
2. *Problems* are often opportunities in disguise. Most innovations are solutions to problems.
3. *Limitations* often reveal opportunities. They help you to see things that you otherwise might miss.

Put those factors together and you get:

$$\text{Problem to Solve} + \text{Limited Resources} + \text{Increasing Passion} = \text{Exponential Innovation}$$

Your greatest ministry innovation could come from your greatest limitation—*if* you have a sincere passion to reach and care for people. When you ask God for eyes to see, you may see what has always been there but you never noticed. Have you ever bought a car and then as you drove it around noticed dozens of other people driving the same car? They were all around you last week; you just didn't have the mindset to see them. Limitations and passion have a way of changing our minds and our eyes.

God did this for us at Life.Church. When our church was

several years old, we built our first building with an auditorium that could seat about six hundred people. Within a year, it was full five times over. In our limited thinking, we had run into a wall. Adding more services seemed impossible. We knew we could not financially afford to build again. Even if we could, it would take way too long. With nowhere to grow, we were afraid we might lose *it*.

That's when God gave us a shot of creativity. Thankfully our team consists of passionate leaders who asked God to transform this obstacle into an opportunity. After praying and brainstorming, someone suggested we consider meeting at a second location. To our knowledge, that had never been done before. (We were unaware that the practice was far from new and was being done around the world.)

Armed with passion, we approached the owner of a movie theater and asked if we could hold worship experiences there on Sundays. This is common practice today, but at the time, the theater had never considered such an option. The owner said yes, and overnight our greatest limitation became the catalyst for what we considered a great innovation: the multisite church.

When people started worshiping at the theater, they found *it*. They excitedly invited others to attend church in such a non-traditional environment. They gave guests every reason to come, explaining that you could eat popcorn in church, sit in comfortable chairs, and even make out in the back row!

God was not finished showing us new things. Shortly after we added this second meeting place, my wife gave birth to our fourth child out of six, Sam. (Yes, I said six. And yes, I love kids. But I *really* love my wife.) Sam was born at four o'clock on a Sunday morning. I knew that if I left my wife at the hospital so I could preach, it could be my last sermon and my kids might grow up as orphans. I would be dead and my wife would be on the run from the police. I panicked. *What are we going to do? We can't get a staff member ready to teach this fast. We can't find a guest preacher at 4:00 a.m.* With no other options, we decided to run the video of the message from Saturday night.

It worked! Why? Because *it* worked! Another obstacle, another innovation: the video message. Those small ideas have enabled us to reach thousands and thousands of people we might not have reached otherwise. If you're facing an obstacle right now, maybe God will increase your passion and give you a breakthrough idea. That breakthrough idea might give your ministry more *it* than ever before.

Leadership guru Peter Drucker said, "An established company which, in an age demanding innovation, is not able to innovate, is doomed to decline and extinction." Though he was referring to businesses, I'd argue this quote applies to churches as well. What obstacle are you facing? Ask God for breakthrough thinking. Don't think about small changes. Think radically. Think out of the box. Destroy the box! Roger Enrico, former chairman of Pepsico, said, "Beware of the tyranny of making small changes to small things. Rather, make big changes to big things." For the sake of those who don't know Christ, think big.

Break the Rules

Most of the greatest spiritual innovators in history were people who broke the rules. Thomas Edison said, "There ain't no rules here. We're trying to accomplish something." People with *it* do life differently than people without it.

No one is a better example than Jesus. By the Pharisees' standards, Jesus failed daily, because they measured success by their rules. He broke the Sabbath. He hung out with the wrong people. His disciples were uneducated. He did things upside down and backward.

And he fulfilled God's perfect will and paid the price for our sins. According to the Pharisees, Jesus failed. According to God, he became the savior of the world.

When you try something new in ministry, most people will tell you your idea will never work. Leadership expert Warren Bennis said, "Innovation . . . by definition will not be accepted at first. It takes repeated attempts, endless demonstrations, monotonous rehearsals before innovation can be accepted and internalized by an organization. This requires *courageous patience*." If you have a God idea, be brave enough to go with it. Break some rules.

Martin Luther broke a big rule. When the church said the common person was not spiritually mature enough to handle the Word of God, Luther disagreed. He broke the rules by innovatively translating the Bible into German and putting it into the hands of the everyday person.

John Wesley broke some rules. It was considered heresy to preach outside of a church building. When he was kicked out of his church, he preached outdoors. His passion to preach Christ, combined with the limited availability of indoor venues, drove him to invent the open-air meeting. This breakthrough opened doors for many others, such as Billy Graham.

Modern-day church leaders continue to break the rules to lead the church in new and innovative ways. Who knows how many people have come to Christ because creative leaders with *it* broke the rules? And who knows how many people may come to Christ if you have the courage to do something that hasn't been done before?

Offended by *It*

As God blesses your ministry with *it*, remember that those without it tend to criticize those with it, especially when you do it differently. Larry Ellison, billionaire and former CEO of the Oracle

Corporation, said, "When you innovate, you've got to be prepared for everyone telling you you're nuts."

Take, for example, the first hot-air balloon. "On June 4, 1783, at the market square of the French village of Annonay, not far from Paris, a smoky bonfire on a raised platform was fed by wet straw and old wool rags. Tethered above, straining its lines, was a huge taffeta bag thirty-three feet in diameter. In the presence of 'a respectable assembly and a great many other people,' and accompanied by great cheering, the balloon was cut from its moorings and set free to rise majestically into the noon sky. Six thousand feet into the air it went—the first public ascent of a balloon, the first step in the history of human flight. It came to earth several miles away in a field, where it was promptly attacked by pitchfork-waving peasants and torn to pieces as an instrument of evil!"[4] Yikes!

Jesus experienced resistance to the irregular almost daily. When he healed a woman who'd been crippled by a spirit for eighteen years, the Pharisees were offended because he did it on the Sabbath. According to Matthew 12, Jesus' healing on the Sabbath motivated the Pharisees to scheme to kill him. That is *unbelievable*. You can't heal on the Sabbath, but you *can* plot murder! If you're going to try something new, get ready to offend some Pharisees.

What's accepted today was often rejected at first. In 1876, Western Union circulated an internal memo which read, "This 'telephone' has too many shortcomings to be seriously considered as a means of communication. The device is of no value to us." Innovations in the Christian community are no exception. So much of what is accepted today was despised just a few years ago. For example, people screamed "heresy" when Martin Luther used the printing press to make the Bible available to the public. Generally accepted practices today, which would have been condemned in many churches just a few decades ago, include dressing casually for church, clapping during worship, and showing videos in a worship service. The innovations of multisite churches and video teaching, church online, and leveraging social media are still despised and rejected by some.

Yesterday's controversy can become today's norm. Today's contemporary becomes tomorrow's traditional. When you have *it*, you'll find new ways to spread it. But be prepared for what goes with it—criticism.

Since preaching Christ tends to bring criticism, I'm not worried when people shoot at me for trying new things. I embrace it as part of what comes with the territory. Do not worry when people criticize you for your boldness to reach others. Worry when they don't. Whatever you do, do not let the rules of people stop you from following God. When he gives *it* to you, go with it.

Too Much of a Good Thing Can Kill *It*

When you have *it*, you might get on a roll with new ideas. But be careful: too much of a good thing can kill *it*.

I worked with the leaders of a great church that unquestionably had *it* for years. During the early days of the church, the people were passionate, generous, committed, and growing spiritually. They brought their friends. Hundreds were saved. They had an impact on the community.

Over time, they built several buildings: phases one, two, and three. As the church grew, instead of using volunteers to lead worship, they hired pros. Rather than enlisting members to stack chairs after church each week, they paid a staff. Instead of preaching passionate and raw messages, the pastor enlisted a research team and used other methods that kept the teaching at arm's length.

Outwardly, they were improved; inwardly, they developed an immunity to the fever that once had driven them. The weekend experiences used to be rougher around the edges. Now they were professionally produced with dress rehearsals and detailed tech and sound checks. Even with all of these "better" tools, the church lost something. The services were slick and well produced, but they lacked what had made them special before. Their *it* had quit.

Kathy Sierra, in her Creating Passionate Users blog, asks, "What makes indie films more appealing than so many of the huge Hollywood productions? What makes indie music more interesting than the slick big-label, big-production records? What's the magic that disappears when you hear the studio-mix version of something you once heard live? Not that most of us have the problem of too big a budget for our own good, but still . . . maybe we should think about whether some imperfections might be a *good* thing. Maybe we should consider whether we're trying too hard to smooth all the rough edges."[5]

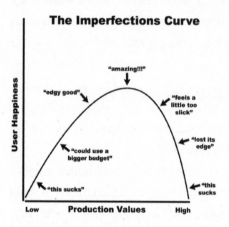

Then she offers what she calls the Imperfections Curve.

Those with *it* grow even more passionate about reaching people. But don't get tricked into trusting your spiritual bells and whistles or you might become too slick, lose your edge, then lose *it*. God doesn't need what many churches think are necessities to reach people. Don't put your faith in the innovations. Keep your faith in Christ.

Tell the Devil to Go to Hell

Tom Kelley starts his book *The Ten Faces of Innovation* with this: "We've all been there. The pivotal meeting where you push forward a new idea or proposal you're passionate about. A fast-paced discussion leads to an upwelling of support that seems about to reach critical mass. And then, in one disastrous moment, your hopes are dashed when someone weighs in with those fatal words: 'Let me just play Devil's Advocate for a minute . . .'"[6] After making that seemingly harmless statement, the person feels free to blast your idea to smithereens. They may say your idea is too far-fetched. Remember, the only reason it seems crazy is because no one has seen it done before.

Your new idea *will* face resistance. It may or may not work. In the next chapter, we'll talk about the necessity of failure on the road to success. Do not let the devil's advocate kill God's plan. Decide today that your team will work together to find new ways to reach people, not more reasons to stay the same. And when someone does try to take the devil's deadly role, tell the devil he can go to hell.

It Factors

- Leaders with *it* do more than just think of new ideas; they actually do the new ideas.
- Innovation is more about mindset than money.
- God often guides by what he doesn't provide.
- Problems are opportunities in disguise.
- A Problem to Solve + Limited Resources + Increasing Passion = Exponential Innovation
- You have everything you need to do what God wants you to do.
- Innovative leaders do anything short of sin to reach the lost.
- "All it takes is one idea to solve an impossible problem" (Robert Schuller).
- Innovation is awesome, but don't put your faith in it. Keep your faith in Christ.

Questions for Discussion or Reflection

1. Many churches make excuses for not trying something new. Some believe they don't have creative people. Others claim they lack resources. Which of these excuses has affected your ministry? Remember, you have everything you need to do what God wants you to do. What resources (people, buildings, technology) are underutilized? What is God showing you?

2. Does your ministry community encourage innovation? If so, what factors drive ministry innovation? If not, what is stopping innovation? What can you do to change the culture and encourage creative forms of ministry?

3. Have you hit something in your ministry that appears to be an obstacle? For the next ten minutes, brainstorm solutions. No idea is a bad idea. During your brainstorming, don't let anyone say, "Yes, but . . ." On every idea that comes up, force people to say, "Yes, and . . ."

4. What idea has been simmering inside you? Is God calling you to do something new that may be hated for a while but changes lives for years to come? What are you going to do about it?

CHAPTER 8

Willingness to Fall Short

*Only those who dare to fail greatly can ever achieve
greatly.*

—Robert F. Kennedy

D o you remember learning to walk? Nope? Me neither. But at
some point, you rolled over for the first time (and I'm sure a
parent screamed with delight). Then you scooted, and later crawled.
Day by day, you attempted new feats only to exceed your previous
accomplishments. Before long, you pulled yourself up on a coffee
table or sofa. Then one day you took the biggest step of your life.
Well, technically at that point it was the *only* step of your life. With
no visible means of support, you took one heck of a step of faith. I
can't speak for you, but every time I watched one of my six kids take
their first step, their eyes always grew huge with a mixture of excitement and fear as they wobbled like a two-foot-tall Frankenstein.
Then, no matter what—whether it was after the first step or the
third—they always fell. Always.

You did the same thing. You don't remember, but you probably
psyched yourself up with some self-help mantra—"What my mind
can conceive, my body can achieve. What my mind can conceive,

my body can achieve"—and then you took a celebratory step and unceremoniously fell. Imagine if following your first tumble, you thought, *Well, that's that. I gave it a shot. Things didn't work out. I'm not meant to be a walker. I guess I'll just crawl the rest of my life.*

That would never happen, but the fear of failure causes many leaders to think with this kind of absurdity. And on they crawl while God wants them to leap and bound.

If you look at any church that has *it*, you will see a church that has failed after many faith-filled attempts. Most of them have failed *often*. Generally these churches are led by aggressive, do-what-it-takes, thick-skinned people who are willing to make mistakes. They know that without faith it is impossible to please God. They understand that faith often requires risk. So what does that mean? You cannot play it safe and please God! Faith in a big God will lead you to take some big risks. These churches' faith makes them not afraid to fail. The fifth leadership ingredient for a church that has *it* and lasts is a willingness to fall short.

In contrast, the ministries without *it* are usually the ones playing it safe, doing only what is sure to succeed. They retreat in fear, never having the faith to walk into something new and unknown.

As counterintuitive as it sounds, failing can often help a ministry experience *it*. Being overly cautious can kill *it*. On the surface, these ideas don't seem to make sense. But they're true. Aggressive leaders with *it* are often dreaming, experimenting, and testing the limits. They don't know what can't be done and are willing to try things others think impossible. Because they know they are more than conquerors through him who loves us, these passionate spiritual entrepreneurs take risks. They are not always successful, failing often. But when they do fail, they tend to rebound quickly. Temporary failures are often followed by lasting success. They try, fail, learn, adjust, and try again. After a series of accidental learning experiences, these hard-hitting leaders often stumble onto innovative ministry ideas they never would have discovered without rolling the dice. As philosopher and educator John Dewey once said, "Failure is instructive. The person who really thinks learns quite as much from his failures as from his successes."

Failing Forward

The person in Scripture who probably best exemplifies the "fail often" principle is Peter. I relate to him because he had great intentions but often messed up in dramatic fashion. Even though he was far from perfect, Peter still had *it*. Perhaps what led Peter to get it, keep it, and spread it was his willingness to fail. If Peter were alive today, he would understand as well as anyone what Walter Brunell meant when he said, "Failure is the tuition you pay for success."

Think about how many times Peter's aggressive nature led to what we could call great learning opportunities. He once offered unsolicited advice to Jesus, insisting that Jesus not give up his life. Jesus, the master teacher, rewarded Peter by calling him Satan. I'm guessing that got Peter's attention. (I have many names I dream of Jesus calling me—friend, son, faithful servant—but Satan is not one of them.)

Another time, Peter hopped out of a boat (while the other eleven disciples played it safe) and walked on water toward Jesus before losing focus and faith and sinking like a, well, *peter* (which in Greek is *petros,* or "rock"). Another great—and wet—lesson.

Then there was the time Jesus was being arrested by a troop of soldiers, and Peter loyally defended him by swinging his sword at the head of a servant of the Jewish high priest (interesting that Peter didn't go after one of the soldiers), slightly missing the center of his target and instead clipping off the poor guy's ear. Again, Jesus offered Peter more valuable instruction.

Soon after, Peter dropped the nuclear bomb of failures when he denied Jesus three times. Luke's gospel shows us what happened after Peter pretended not to even know Jesus. "The Lord turned and looked straight at Peter. Then Peter remembered the word the Lord had spoken to him: 'Before the rooster crows today, you will disown me three times'" (Luke 22:61). Peter had pledged his undying loyalty to Jesus, even pushing off the other disciples, claiming that *he* would always stand by Jesus even if the others didn't. Then Peter cowered and hid, not even making a show of support at the cross as Jesus gave his life.

It was a failure, but it was also an opportunity for growth.

The full impact of this lesson sank in for Peter only after the resurrection, when Jesus forgave him and restored him to a position of huge responsibility. Think about that. It's not normally the way we reward failures, but God is different. When Jesus rose from the dead and forgave Peter, this disciple would never be the same.

Peter's education consisted of trying, failing, learning, adjusting, and trying again. His "failing forward" most likely contributed to God's decision to choose Peter as the guest speaker on the day of Pentecost. Can you imagine anyone preaching with more passion than the guy who was forgiven after denying Jesus three times?

Peter learned from his failures. Then he told people to repent of their sins, and he led three thousand people to Christ and helped birth the church. Peter failed often. But he still had *it*.

> We take risks not only because they might pay off but also because when we fail, we fail forward.

We take risks not only because they might pay off but also because when we fail, we fail forward.

As a marketing major in college, I was trained to get people's attention. This asset became a curse when I unintentionally hurt some church leaders with a billboard campaign targeted at the unchurched. This is one of my more embarrassing moments as a church leader. I regret that we did it, but I cannot change what we did.

Our outreach strategy included billboards that read, "Think church is boring and outdated? So did we." Another one said, "Hate church? So did we." Each statement was followed by the line "Lifechurch.tv—not what you'd expect." (Lifechurch.tv is not our name anymore. Another embarrassing season. But we'll save that story for another book.) Although these signs drew the attention of our target crowd, they also drew fire from an unintended group— other churches. In my heart, I wasn't taking shots at other churches. Yet other leaders took offense. When I put myself in their shoes, I understood why. I had to admit my mistake and learn from it. Now I'm careful to build up other churches and strive never to make another ministry look bad.

Those who fail forward can relate to Michael Jordan, one of the greatest basketball players of all time, who said, "I've missed more than nine thousand shots in my career. I've lost almost three hundred games. Twenty-six times, I've been trusted to take the game-winning shot and missed. I've failed over and over and over again in my life. And that is why I succeed."

Failing Past Your Local Max

Seth Godin writes in his book *Small Is the New Big* about the idea of a "local max." He explains that when an organization is struggling to move forward, its leaders are likely trying to understand the true nature of peak performance.

Godin explains, "Everyone starts at that dot at the bottom left corner. You're not succeeding at this point, simply because you haven't

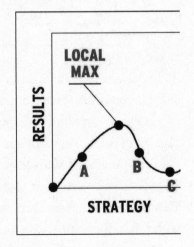

started yet. Then you try something. If it works, you end up at point A . . . Of course, being a success-oriented capitalist, that's not enough. So you do more. You push and hone and optimize until you end up at the Local Max. The Local Max is where your efforts really pay off. So you try even harder. And you end up at point B. Point B is a bummer. Point B is *backward*. Point B is where more effort doesn't return better results anymore. So, you retreat. You go back to your Local Max."[7]

By "local max," Godin seems to mean the place of your most comfortable success. With some effort and a little bit of brain power, you find that you can continue to produce consistent results relatively easily.

In the church world, this is where many people stay. To move past the local max is risky. You'll likely make some mistakes, fail, and struggle. That's scary, so most stick with what they know. They stay at their local max. But according to Godin, the local max chart is incomplete. The chart really looks like this:

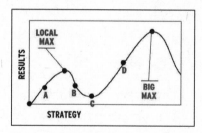

Big max is what you want! The difference between your local max and the big max may be one or two failures followed by seasons of learning. *It* is not that far away.

The problem is you have to go through point C. Point C includes some failure, even a time of reduced results. Those who lack *it* are afraid of C. Disheartened by setbacks, they pull back and start avoiding risks. They slide back to their former place of mastery. They stop growing as leaders and freeze in time.

But the leaders with *it* push through the failures. They know setbacks can be setups for better things to come. They study their failures and learn from them. No one enjoys failing, but when those with *it* fail, they think in terms of failing forward.

Failure Is Not an Option

One church I've followed had *it* for years. This unique and special ministry was built by leaders who failed often. These brave spiritual pioneers rolled the dice, often seeming to lose their gambles. But with each failure, the entrepreneurial leaders learned, adjusted, and attacked again. They discovered new ways of doing ministry and set an example for churches around the world.

One day this church realized they had accomplished a lot. They had churches across the world looking to them, following their every move. Feeling the weight of being such a respected example, the leaders grew more and more cautious. Within a few years, these formerly most daring of Christian leaders were playing it safe.

I once met with a few of these greats, and I tossed out a few off-the-wall ideas. One of them explained to me, in a tone that almost seemed apologetic, "Craig, when you get to where we are, you can't afford to make mistakes. For us, failure is not an option."

My heart broke. These were my heroes. They had mortgaged their homes for the vision of the church. They had endured harsh criticism for their ministry experiments. They had broken new ground. They blazed new trails. Sometimes they succeeded, but often they failed. When they failed, they learned and grew. They broke through ceilings. They busted barriers. They shattered paradigms. They led the way for thousands to follow. They had *it* like few other churches I'd known. Now they were starting to lose it.

This leader's quote is stuck in my mind: "Failure is not an option." I agree wholeheartedly. In our meetings, I repeat it to our staff over and over again, with a little twist: "Failure is not an option. *It is essential.*"

> "Failure is not an option. *It is essential.*"

Those who have *it* usually grow to understand that failure is a part of success. Businessman and author Robert T. Kiyosaki said, "Winners are not afraid of losing. But losers are. Failure is part of the process of success. People who avoid failure also avoid success." Because great leaders are innovative, they are also often scared. That doesn't stop them. They know the path to their greatest potential is often straight through their greatest fear. They are betting the farm. They're swinging for the fence. Those who swing hard will strike out often. But they will also knock some out of the park.

For the record, my friends at the church who decided they would never fail—they are starting to fail again. And guess what? They're starting to succeed in new ways. The church world is watching and celebrating as this church that once had it, and started to lose it, is getting it back again.

Ready, Set, Fail

As you seek God and he ignites it in your heart, I believe he is going to speak to you. Maybe he already has. He is directing you to step out of your comfort zone and do something that takes faith. If he hasn't yet, he will soon. When he does, mark my words, your spiritual enemy, the father of lies, will try to talk you out of it.

One of the devil's greatest tools is fear. You might ask, "How do I overcome this fear of failure?" I like what my friend Mark Batterson says about fear: "The antidote for the fear of failure is not success but small doses of failure." Think about it. To keep you from getting the flu, what kind of shot does the doctor give you? He gives you a small dose of the flu. You get just enough to train your body to reject it. The same is true with failure. Once you fail and realize that failing is not the end of the world, you're not as afraid to fail again. Author, speaker, and professor Leo F. Buscaglia said it well: "We seem to gain wisdom more readily through our failures than through our successes. We always think of failure as the antithesis of success, but it isn't. Success often lies just the other side of failure."

God gave me the great gift of failure early in the ministry. Much of what I tried failed. Our drama ministry fell apart. Our attempt at a choir didn't work. Our first missions trip didn't happen. Our Wednesday Bible study crashed before takeoff. Our monthly worship night happened only twice. We tried a very simple sermon illustration during which Sam Roberts was supposed to toss me a football. We practiced dozens of times. On "game day," in front of the whole church, he threw a wild pass and I dove for it, missing the ball and crashing into the drum set. Pass incomplete. The dumbest failure? We sent out twenty thousand mailers inviting people to our church. Only problem was we didn't put the address of the church on it. (I could not make this up.)

Much of what we have tried failed. Most people just don't know that.

One of the things our church is known for is meeting in multiple locations. Our first attempt at a video venue was a disaster. After struggling for four months, we pulled the plug. Then in 2005, we attempted two church campuses one thousand miles across the country. At the time, we had five or six churches meeting in Oklahoma. Suddenly we decided it would be amazing to start two (not one, but two!) in Phoenix, Arizona. Were any of us from Phoenix? No. Did we understand the culture? No. Had we been to Phoenix? Yes. (We were not that stupid.) But I had been only one time, and it was to attend a conference. (So maybe we were that stupid.)

We started with those bad billboards. (Why not make friends with other churches while we were new in town?) Then we launched in two school gyms on opposite sides of town. We had seven hundred or so people at both locations before our Gideon revival started. (If you don't know what a Gideon revival is, that is when you grow *backward.*) When it became obvious both could not survive, we combined the two into one campus and hoped for the best.

A couple of painful years later, we called it quits. Neither campus survived. We were totally embarrassed. Not only did our whole church know about our failure, so did many other church leaders who were watching. We wasted so much energy and money. That was *God's* money we flushed down the toilet. Even worse, we unintentionally hurt and disappointed people. It was hard to explain how we could invite people to give their hearts to our church and then close the church location.

We tried, we failed, we learned. It was an expensive and painful education. But it was a valuable one. What we learned from that failure would have been difficult to learn any other way. Although I never want to go through a season like that again, those mistakes helped us. They taught us what works and what doesn't work. The lessons we learned from those failures became the foundation for our impact today. Now our church meets not just in Oklahoma but in Texas, Arkansas, Kansas, Missouri, Nebraska, Florida, New Mexico, New York, Tennessee, Iowa, and Colorado. We try to follow Irish writer Samuel Beckett's advice: "Go on failing. Go on. Only next time, try to fail better." You could say we have failed our way to success.

If you don't have *it,* maybe you need to try something new—and fail at it. At our church, we want to give our leaders two gifts: the freedom to fail and the room to rise. I often tell our staff, "Fail! If you're not failing, you've stopped dreaming. You'll eventually stop learning. And you will stop growing."

Those who have *it* fail often.

The Virtue of the Twice Stung

One day, I was walking outside my house and got stung on the back of the head by a wasp. I cried like a four-year-old girl. (Actually, most little kids would handle it better than I did.) Now each time I walk by that spot, I hesitate.

Too many ministry leaders are hesitant. It's easy to understand why. They have tried something that did not work as they expected. They've faced ridicule and gossip and perhaps have even been asked to leave their ministry roles. They've been stung once, and they go out of their way to avoid a repeat.

When you fail, you tend to second-guess yourself. *Maybe I didn't hear from God. Maybe I'm not gifted in ministry. Maybe I'll always fail. I don't think I have what it takes.* Fight against that hesitant-leader syndrome. Sure, you will want to be prayerful and wise as you move forward. Yes, you'll always want to consider the cost before launching a new ministry effort. But remember the words of the writer of Hebrews: "And without faith it is impossible to please God" (Heb. 11:6). God is calling you to risk being stung again. And again. And to recognize that this is the best way to live, the only way to please him.

If you're waiting for your venture to have guaranteed success, you will probably be waiting for the rest of your life. Sometimes the fruit of your steps of faith is measured not so much by what God does *through* you as by what God does *in* you.

As I'm writing this chapter, we just shut down a significant ministry. I mentioned our new venture, the Bible Lens app. I didn't mention that I had bragged about it to about 350,000 people at the Global Leadership Summit. That just makes the failure sting even more. We failed, very publicly, again. So what did we do next? We asked lots of questions so we could learn from our mistake. Next time, we will be smarter, better, and wiser. (And I likely won't announce big untested ventures at leadership conferences anymore!)

I've got another idea I'm playing with right now. It's different. It's risky. It is a potential game changer for churches. Then again, maybe I'm wrong. We'll never know until we try.

Dig Up Your Talent

Jesus told a story in Matthew 25 about three household managers whose master entrusted them with "talents." (Not to be confused with our English word *talent*, a talent was a unit of gold or silver, worth quite a bit in that day.) Two of the guys risked failure and invested their master's money. The third guy was afraid and refused to fail. He played it safe, avoided risk, and buried his talent—just like so many leaders and ministries do today.

Then the master came back and called his employees to report on their investments: "The man who had received the one talent [the guy who feared failure] came. 'Master,' he said, 'I knew that you are a hard man . . . So I was *afraid* and went out and hid your talent in the ground. See, here is what belongs to you.'

"His master replied, 'You wicked, lazy servant! . . . Take the talent from him and give it to the one who has the ten talents'" (Matt. 25:24–28 NIV 1984, emphasis mine).

Luke 19 tells a similar story. *The Message* version offers this summary in verse 26: "Risk your life and get more than you ever dreamed of. Play it safe and end up holding the bag." Those who risked saw an increase. The one who played it safe lost it all.

What dream have you buried? What burden has God given you that you've put aside? Dig it up. Pull it out. Dust it off. It's time to start praying about your next risk.

Is God calling you to start a new ministry? Maybe it's a Saturday-evening worship experience? Or a second location? A missions outreach? A new church? An online ministry?

Perhaps God is calling you to take a chance on a person. To add to your ministry team someone who most think is unqualified. To reach out to someone who is far from God.

Or could it be God is leading you to take a risk and shut down a struggling ministry? Perhaps you know God wants you to have a tough conversation with someone. Maybe he's leading you to find a new place to use your gifts.

It's time to dig up your talent—the assets God has entrusted to you to use for his purposes.

Remember, when you take a step of faith, the fear of failure might creep up on you, as it does with most people. *What if this doesn't work? What will people think? What if this bombs?* I can relate. I feel those fears. One of my mentors told me, "When you believe God is calling you to do something, you have to feel the fear and do it anyway" (my paraphrase).

Let God turn the fear into faith. Instead of becoming a hesitant leader, ask God to make you bold and aggressive.

Ministry without Regrets

When my son Sam was two years old, I stupidly put him on a scooter and let him ride down our steep driveway with me. We took dozens of successful rides together, screaming with joy as we flew down the steep driveway. Lots of two-year-olds would be too afraid. Not Sam. Internally I beamed with pride, thinking, *Yep. A chip off the old block.*

On our final ride, Sam panicked and stepped off the scooter, snapping his femur in two. I heard it crack. It was my fault, a consequence of my poor judgment. He screamed and screamed in horror and pain. Little Sam spent the next six weeks in a full body cast. Once the cast was removed, it took him weeks to learn to walk again.

From that moment forward, Sam was understandably terrified of the steep incline down the driveway. (Yes, I know horrible parenting caused that. Yes, I've changed my ways.) The driveway, though, was only the secondary monster. The big, hairy, super-scary monster was the scoot-scoot, his name for his archenemy.

Sam would walk on the other side of the garage just so the scoot-scoot didn't "get him."

You can imagine my shock a couple of years later when Sam bravely approached me and told me he *had* to ride the scoot-scoot down the driveway. I could tell he was paralyzed with fear but wanted to face and overcome it. I told him firmly, "No, it's not worth it. It's not going to happen." The more I told him no, the more Sam insisted. "You don't understand, Daddy," he pleaded. "I *have* to do it." There was something in his tone, a quiet resolve that made me pause. It was then I realized that Sam had something to prove—not to me but to himself.

For quite some time, he stood at the top of the driveway holding the scooter and staring down as if at potential doom. Crying quietly, breathing deeply, and preparing to face his greatest fear, Sam took one deep breath after another, talking courage to himself like a warrior preparing for battle. After several false starts, Sam pushed off and soared down the driveway. At the bottom, he roared in victory and spiked scoot-scoot like a wide receiver spikes a football in the end zone after a game-winning catch. Sam had risked and won! I may never be more proud of him. That was a ride he had to take, a fear he had to conquer.

What ride do you need to take?

Learning to Fail Gracefully

Stuntmen and stuntwomen are paid to fail. They fall and get beat up and get blown up—gracefully. We need to learn to fail gracefully.

Because I've failed often, I've learned some principles about how to fail. Here are a few you might find helpful:

1. *Call your new ideas experiments.* Sometimes leaders make promises they might not be able to deliver on. Instead of

making absolute statements about what's coming, it helps to package new ventures as experiments. This gives leaders some wiggle room to make minor tweaks or major adjustments. If the experiment doesn't work, we still come away with something valuable, something we've learned and can explain to those concerned.

2. *Create a culture that allows for failure.* Explain to your team that failure is a part of success. Talk openly about your failures and what you've learned. Tell them that, as a ministry, you're going to err on the side of being aggressive and failing occasionally, rather than being passive and succeeding at being average.

   For instance, I once had an assistant who was overly cautious. I challenged her to make three aggressive failures in the next quarter. I told her that instead of my "pressing the pedal" to get her to accelerate, I'd prefer she make me "use the brakes" occasionally.

   We will always make mistakes. I'd rather we make aggressive ones than passive ones. I think the greatest regrets we have are not failures but risks we didn't take. We need to help our team know that mistakes are part of progress and that failure is allowed.

3. *Don't internalize failures.* Motivational speaker Zig Ziglar said, "Failure is an event, not a person." When you fail, allow yourself to feel the disappointment. That's reality, and an important part of it. Feel disappointment, but don't internalize disapproval.

   Thomas Edison failed repeatedly but said, "I have not failed. I've just found 10,000 ways that won't work." Can you imagine if his ineffective early attempts had led him to decide he was incapable? He never would have invented the lightbulb!

Failing at something does not make you a failure. Shake it off. Learn from it. Try something again. Yes, you are going to feel unsure of yourself and unsure of your idea, but if you wait until you are 100 percent sure to try something new, you will almost always be too late. So go for it.

4. *Debrief after failures and successes.* Instead of living in denial about disappointing new ventures, take time to debrief. List the learning points. What worked? What didn't? What could you have done differently? What are the lessons you'll carry forward? Don't waste a setback by not learning from it.

5. *Try again.* If you fall off your scooter, get back on it and ride again. Don't let yesterday's loss talk you out of tomorrow's win. Try again. God's not finished with you. Most big successes follow multiple failures. Winston Churchill said, "Success consists of going from failure to failure without loss of enthusiasm."

The greatest regrets we have are not failures but risks we didn't take. Can you imagine paying for something and then not getting what you paid for? Perhaps you can. Maybe you have gone through a drive-through, driven away, and then discovered you didn't get one of the items you ordered. Ugh! Failure is often the price you pay for success. Don't fail and then not get what you paid for. Try again!

Get Out of the Boat

You have to take risks to get *it* and keep it. That means you have to make a choice. As leaders, we often fear failure more than anything else. But our greatest pain is regret. That's why you have to make some faith-filled choices. You can avoid risks, minimize the downside, and continue to play it safe. But you also give up the upside and you will never know what might have been had you developed the faith to try. To continue to have *it,* you have to face your fears or you will likely end up with regrets.

When you lead on the edge, you learn to face your fears and conquer them, only to have new ones emerge. You learn that the illusion of security evaporates with your last accomplishment. But like Peter, you recognize you're safer when you are out of the boat and *with Jesus* than if your fears keep you in the boat.

Get out of the boat. Face your fears. Fail. Learn. Adjust. Try again. And watch God do more than you can imagine.

It Factors

- Failure is not an option. It is a necessity.
- If you're not failing, you've stopped dreaming. You'll eventually stop learning and you will stop growing. Those who have *it* fail often.
- It is impossible to please God without faith, which means we have to risk.
- Sometimes the fruit of your steps of faith is measured not so much by what God does through you as by what God does in you.
- Failure is often the tuition for success (adapted from Walter Brunell).
- Debrief after you fail so it becomes a learning experience.
- If you're breathing, God's not finished with you.
- If you've failed, you have learned something others haven't and are in the perfect position to try again and succeed.
- Great leaders learn the art of failing forward.
- The pain of regret is often greater than the pain of failure. So get out of the boat.

Questions for Discussion or Reflection

1. Describe the "failure culture" at your ministry. Is strategic failure strongly discouraged, quietly tolerated, or publicly embraced?

2. Is your ministry becoming more faith filled or more risk averse? When is the last time you took a huge faith risk? What happened? What did you learn?

3. *The Message* version of the Bible offers this summary in Luke 19:26: "Risk your life and get more than you ever dreamed of. Play it safe and end up holding the bag." In light of this verse, what is God saying to you about your ministry? How are you playing it safe? What risk is God calling you to take? What will you regret if you don't at least try?

4. Great leaders often ask, "What would you attempt if you knew it couldn't fail?" Talk with your team about this. If you knew that God would bless anything that you do, what would you attempt?

CHAPTER 9

Hearts Focused Outward

If your gospel isn't touching others, it hasn't touched you.

—Curry R. Blake

Something I saw years ago still breaks my heart. I was preaching for a small church across town. The volunteer receptionist told me bluntly before the service started, "Young man, you'd better do a good job preaching, because we have a visitor coming to church." Evidently having a guest visit the church was unusual. She explained that a lady had just called and asked for directions to the church. "Our church has been declining for several years," the receptionist said sadly, "and we need members to help keep the doors open."

Before the service started, I stood outside the front door with a church bouncer (uh, sorry, I mean church elder). We were greeting people, and then I saw her. *The visitor.* The reason I knew this woman wasn't a member of the church was, well, because she didn't look like anyone else. All the members were dressed in nice suits and pretty dresses. This young lady looked like she'd slept in what she was wearing. It wasn't that she didn't care for herself; it was just obvious that she was in a tough season in life. As she slowly approached the church, her eyes and body language communicated she was nervous and intimidated. I admired her courage to visit a new church all by herself. What had triggered her to come? Had she been abused? Abandoned? Was she at the end of her rope and in desperate need of hope?

The elder stepped in front of the young lady, blocking her path into the sanctuary. "Miss," the man said in an intimidating tone, "at our church, we wear our best for God."

My jaw dropped in shock. *No! You didn't just say that to her.* Unfortunately, he had. This young woman's eyes filled with tears as she dashed to her car to make her getaway.

Heartbreaking.

I'd argue that many people today are not rejecting Christ so much as they are rejecting the church. Perhaps more specifically, they are rejecting judgmental Christians. Once, I asked a guy why he didn't go to church. He responded without hesitation, "Because I've already been."

He went to a church. *It* didn't happen. He never returned.

Have you ever visited a church and been left out or overlooked? It makes you feel incredibly uncomfortable and unwanted. What's odd is that churches that appear unfriendly to outsiders can be full of the friendliest people in the world. But only if you're an insider.

Churches without this leadership ingredient can be so tight, so bonded, so close—to each other—that they unintentionally overlook those they don't know. They are welcoming, warm, and hospitable—to their own. But if you are from the outside or look different because of your clothes or your tattoos, you might be ignored or even shunned.

Ministries with *it* remember that Jesus came for outsiders. He came for those who were lost. Broken. Hurting. Disenfranchised. Alone. Overlooked. Poor. Jesus came for those whom religion rejected. Many churches unknowingly focus inward, forgetting the people who need

Jesus the most. These churches are like a hospital that no longer accepts patients. Or a soup kitchen that no longer feeds hungry people. Or like SpongeBob no longer wearing square pants. (I may have given one metaphor too many there.)

Ministries with *it* remember that Jesus came for outsiders.

Examine a church that leads like *it* matters, and you'll find a virtual obsession with reaching people who don't know Christ. They don't add to their mission. Helping people find new life *is* their mission. A passion to share Christ consumes them in a beautiful way.

Churches without *it* are often filled with sincere Bible-believing Christians. Unfortunately, they're simply more concerned about themselves than about people who are not yet Christians and don't yet believe the Bible. They love the comfort of their Christian bubble so much they're not willing to follow Jesus as he tries to lead them to become friends with sinners so they can seek and save the lost.

Who Do You Love?

Once, a guy asked Jesus, "Of all the commands, what's the big one?"

Jesus replied, "'*Love* the Lord your God with all your heart and with all your soul and with all your mind and with all your strength.' The second is this: '*Love* your neighbor as yourself'" (Mark 12:30–31, emphases mine).

Who do *you* love? If you love God, you should love people. If you do not love people, you do not love God. "Anyone who loves is a child of God and knows God. But anyone who does not love does not know God; for God is love. . . . If we don't love people we can see, how can we love God, whom we cannot see?" (1 John 4:7–8, 20 NLT). It's that simple.

We're quite comfortable loving those who are like us, but we're also called to love those who aren't like us, and we are especially called to love those who are far from God.

When we love deeply, love leads us to do things we wouldn't otherwise do. For example, I'm a cheapo, but I'll spend big bucks on a date with my wife. What makes me do it? Love makes me do it.

Another example: I dislike most cats. (I'm trying to be polite.) My kids love cats. So for almost twenty years, we hosted two fur-ball-spitting, never-come-when-you-call-them, ignore-you-all-day-and-wake-you-up-at-three-in-the-morning cats. Why did I have two of something I don't enjoy? Because I love my kids. Love made me do it.

When one of my kids asked me yesterday for the last one of my favorite drink, I gave it to him. Love made me do it.

Years ago, when my son Stephen was a toddler and pooped all over himself, and his sister saw it and then vomited her dinner of spaghetti with meatballs directly onto the freshly squeezed-out poop, I cleaned it all up. What made me do it? Well, actually *Amy* made me do that, but you get the point.

Love makes you do crazy things. Who do you love? Do you love people who don't know Christ? The it-fueled do, and deeply.

But honestly, many so-called Christians don't. You do not have to look far to find churches full of people who are insulating themselves from the world, hunkering down, avoiding popular movies and secular music. These inward-looking religious types keep their distance from anyone who drinks beer, cusses after a bad golf swing, smokes anything, has a tattoo, listens to rap music, or wears jeans with holes in them. They judge people who voted differently. They criticize rock stars. They stay away from people of a different color of skin. They stare disapprovingly at purple hair and mohawks. They're afraid of bars, rock concerts, and some social-media sites.

Too many believers are avoiding "that kind" of person. Somehow they've forgotten Jesus came for that kind of person.

Do you love people who are without Christ? Be honest. Does your ministry have people whose hearts beat for those outside the family of God? Churches that have *it* care for each other *and* for people who are far from God. Churches and ministries without *it* care more about the sheep inside the fold than the goats outside of the church. That lack of caring is communicated clearly. One church I visited has a beautiful stained-glass window inscribed with the verse "Jesus is the light of the world." The only problem is that the words were facing people inside the church instead of people who observed the message from the outside.

What caused the good shepherd to leave the ninety-nine to pursue the one that was lost? Love. What made the father stand on the front porch waiting, hoping, and praying that his lost son would return home? Love. What drove our heavenly Father from heaven to earth? Love again. John 3:16 records his motivation: "For God so *loved* the world that he gave his one and only Son, that whoever believes in him shall not perish but have eternal life" (emphasis mine). What empowered Jesus to suffer greatly, to shed his innocent blood, and to willingly offer his life? Love made him do it.

Do you love the lost?

Churches that have *it* care for each other *and* for people who are far from God.

An Open-Roof Policy

Life in Palestine in Jesus' day was very public. People generally left their doors open during the day. An open door meant anyone could enter.

One day in Capernaum, Jesus started teaching inside an open-doored house, and his followers barged right on in. Soon the tiny house was packed like a can of sardines and people overflowed into the streets. (Jesus could have gone to two services or started a second campus. Too bad we were not there to advise him.)

We know that out of the entire crowd, at least four guys had *it*. These fanatical four had a crippled friend who desperately needed

Jesus. They were on a mission not to get a selfie with the Savior but to get their friend to Christ.

What about the rest of the crowd? Some were probably sincere in their desire to hear Jesus. Others might have been skeptical, hoping to prove Jesus was a fake. But these four friends were thinking about someone else. Even though others might have hung on Jesus' words, many missed the heart of his message. Jesus did not come for the healthy but for the sick.

For the crowd, the meeting was about them. What could they get? What could they learn? What could Jesus offer them? Churches without *it* are filled with well-meaning Christians with similar attitudes. You hear it in their self-centered words:

- We love this church because it is close to our home.
- We go to this church because our kids love the day care.
- We enjoy going early for the free coffee and donuts.
- This church makes me feel better about myself.

You hear it in their language when they're searching for a church home. "We're church shopping," they might say. We know what they mean, but their words imply they are consumers looking for a church to meet their needs. When they find a church they like, they choose it. If one day this church is no longer doing it for them, they leave, singing the national anthem of consumeristic church hoppers: "We're just not getting fed. We're not getting fed. We're going to leave every church in town and we won't stop until we're dead." Pastor Erwin McManus asked, "When have we forgotten that the church doesn't exist for us? We are the church, and we exist for the world."

Turning Outward

If your ministry has become focused on the already convinced, it is a safe bet your ministry doesn't have *it*. You are not likely seeing many, if any, new people come to faith in Christ. Baptisms are few and far between. Membership classes are tiny. You're not experiencing great works of the Spirit of God. New people aren't coming and staying and inviting others to join the spiritual ride. Longtime members aren't growing. Things may be stable, but they are spiritually stagnant. You are not seeing forward movement.

We can learn a few things from these four men. For starters, to have *it,* we have to care about people who are far from God. Many people don't.

I heard a story about a preacher correcting his inward-looking church. "The problem," the preacher's voice boomed, "is that people are dying all over the world and you don't even give a damn!" When he punched the final word, the crowd gasped. Women looked at each other, stunned. Kids sat at attention, afraid to budge. The elders eyed one another, sending silent but understood messages: *We have to meet. Soon.*

The minister continued, much more slowly and with obvious pain. "The saddest part is . . ." He paused and started again. "The saddest part is that most of you are more upset that I used the word *damn* in church than you are that people are dying and going to hell."

Ouch.

As my close friend Pastor Vince Antonucci asks, "Are you close to people who are far from God? If you're not close to people who are far from God, you're not as close to God as you think you are. Because God's heart is always with people who are far from him."

Ouch again.

Do you care about those who are without Christ? Before you give me the programmed churchy answer most Christians give, let me help you answer this question honestly.

- When is the last time you've had a lost person in your
  home? (The plumber who repaired your sink doesn't count.)

- How many meaningful conversations did you have with non-Christians this week?
- When is the last time you talked about your faith with someone far from God?
- Who are the nonbelievers you prayed for today?

If you can't answer those questions with several stories or people's names, chances are you are on the road to not caring. Perhaps you have already arrived and have settled in at that dangerous destination. To be fair, most Christians don't wake up one morning and declare, "I have decided not to care about the lost anymore." The attitude creeps in over time. After being a Christian for a few years, we don't have a ton in common with non-Christians, so we typically don't develop quality relationships with them. Over time, many Christ followers realize they have almost no close or even developing relationships with unbelievers.

If that is you, ask God to break your heart for those without Christ. He will. Before long, God will send you someone—maybe a bunch of someones—whom you will grow to care about. Your love for them will increase. When that happens, you get *it*, and it's almost impossible to turn off. Your passion to pray grows. You start looking for opportunities to shift conversations toward spiritual things. You become ever aware that you are representing Christ. When you have *it*, people tend to want it. Your passion for Jesus and his mission becomes contagious.

I bumped into two wonderfully obnoxious guys. Unquestionably, they have *it*. Both guys talked simultaneously, describing the Bible study they were having in a restaurant. After too many refills of Diet Coke, these two went to the men's room and were still talking about Jesus while "taking care of business." Two other guys overheard their conversation. Before long, these bathroom evangelists led the other two guys in a prayer to know Christ—right in the men's restroom! Their new friends followed them back to their table and enjoyed the remainder of the Bible study. Now the new believers are regulars at the study gatherings.

For too many years, I was not focused on sharing Christ. Like many, I got distracted, consumed by my own problems. Life became about me. I needed to reconnect with Jesus and have him reignite my evangelistic flame. I asked and he answered. Now that I have *it* again, God seems to be bringing people to me. Like a trainer I often see at the gym. This guy knows I'm a pastor but does not hold back using the f-bomb around me. He drops cuss words like a rapper drops rhymes. The other day, I was ready to work out, but I could tell he needed to talk. In the past, I might have been selfish and politely brushed him off so I could commence sweating. But I knew God wanted me to slow down and continue the conversation with this guy.

Moments later, the trainer, whom I barely knew, shared how his girlfriend had cheated on him. Before I could bring up anything spiritual, he asked if I would pray for him. After our prayer, I talked to him about Jesus. He was curious but had some reservations about Christianity because of a bad experience with some Christians. I invited him to church. He said sincerely, "That's what I need to do."

If you are a leader of your ministry, you need to recognize that, for better or for worse, your ministry reflects you. If you do not care about Christ-less lives, the people you lead are likely not to care. Well-known preaching professor Howard Hendricks said, "In the midst of a generation screaming for answers, Christians are stuttering."

Lessons from Four Homewreckers

Many churches unintentionally turn their backs on people who need Jesus most. We focus inward. We do our Bible studies. We listen to our favorite Christian music. We watch our Christian shows.

We speak our Christianese. *Praise the Lord, brother. Thank God I'm blood bought, sanctified, Spirit filled, and glory bound!* And we are basically saying to those who need him most, "You can just go to hell." I know that is not what we're *actually* saying, but if we are not careful, that is what our uncaring attitudes will communicate.

Here are a few things we should learn from the fervent, fixated, friend-toting four of Capernaum. First, they recognized their friend needed Jesus. Too many believers forget that the lost *really* need Jesus. You can see it in what I call "good-old-boy theology." I can't tell you how many times I've visited a family in which someone just passed away and I ask about their deceased loved one. The family shuffles back and forth awkwardly before saying, "Well, Grandpa wasn't much of a churchgoer and he definitely wasn't religious, but he was a hard worker, and besides his gambling problem and the fact that he ordered himself a strip-o-gram for his eightieth birthday, he was a pretty moral person. We know he's in a better place." We want to believe people we love never go to hell. We can always talk ourselves into believing people are better off now that they're gone, and it lessens our urgency to reach those without Christ.

We also see that it took four people to get the one man to Jesus. A church that has *it* recognizes that reaching people is not just the pastor's job. It's everyone's job. I can't do it alone. You can't do it alone. It takes all of us.

> A church that has *it* recognizes that reaching people is not just the pastor's job. It's everyone's job.

It takes all of us—and God. So many don't do evangelism because they feel like they are not qualified to lead someone to Jesus. Good news: God will lead the person to Jesus through you.

If you're anything like me, you might feel nervous in spiritual conversations. In seminary, I took a class on personal evangelism. We had to go door to door and knock and try to lead the unsuspecting person—who was probably traumatized by being faced with some young seminarian ready to talk about hell while a teacher looked over his shoulder to grade him—to Christ. My professor always reminded us to pray before we knocked. I always pleaded, "God, I pray no one is home!" Why? Because I was nervous. I never felt like I'd do it right.

We have to remember, we do our part, others do their part, and God does his part. We are never the answer; Jesus always is.

I know many pastors who are afraid to ask people to put their faith in Jesus in their church services. They worry no one will respond. I always tell young ministers, "You don't fail if the Spirit prompts you to ask someone to follow Christ and the person doesn't. You fail when the Spirit prompts you but you're too afraid to ask." Don't blame yourself if someone rejects Jesus. That's putting you in God's place.

Outreach is a team event. You might be just one of the four. Your position might be pray-er. You are the behind-the-scenes intercessor. Or maybe you are the conversationalist. You naturally engage and help explain the gospel. Or you are simply a love-of-Jesus gooddoer. Your actions speak louder than most people's words. God might put you in for the first quarter, then let you watch from the bench while others perform their specialties. You do your part. Let others do theirs. Watch God do his.

Cutting Through the Crap

The four guys with *it* were determined to do everything necessary to get their crippled friend to Jesus. As they approached the home where Jesus was teaching, they couldn't get in because the crowd was way too big. Undeterred by that little problem, the four amigos decided to bust him in, so they climbed up onto the roof of the house. The roofs on these homes typically were flat with beams about three feet apart. The gaps between the beams were covered with brush and clay and packed with manure. You read that right. Manure.

Imagine the scene: Jesus is teaching. I mean, he's in it, on a roll, flowin' with the Spirit. A flake of dried poop lands on his head. He looks up and the ceiling starts caving in. The homeowner is not exactly pleased. Suddenly the light of the sun explodes through a gaping hole, shining around the silhouettes of four guys leaning over and staring down at everyone. Jesus starts laughing with delight.

These guys were willing to bust through any barriers. They even dug through the manure.

Churches that have *it* are filled with people who sincerely desire to reach the lost. They won't let any excuses stop them. Crowd blocking the path? No problem. They'll go over, under, around, or through it. Roof in the way? Nothing stands in the way of *it*. They'll cut through the roof.

Love overcomes the obstacles.

The first thing Jesus did was to heal the crippled man's greatest brokenness. Jesus forgave his sins. Yes, that's right. Before Jesus healed the man, Jesus gave him an even greater gift. Jesus offered him grace. Then Jesus said to the paralytic, "'I tell you, get up, take your mat and go home.' He got up, took his mat and walked out in full view of them all. This amazed everyone and they praised God, saying, 'We have never seen anything like this!'" (Mark 2:11–12).

You know your ministry has *it* when people start talking like the people in this story. They tell everyone, "We've never seen anything like this!"

Shifting the Focus Outward

If your ministry doesn't have *it* and you want it, shifting to an outward, evangelistic focus is essential. Let's keep things simple.

What does it take for you to see people come to Christ? I'd say three things. Let's break them down to understand the importance of each.

1. People Who Don't Know Christ

To see people come to Christ in your ministry, you need to have people present who don't know him. That might seem obvious, but it's worth stating. Ask yourself honestly, do people who are not yet Christians feel welcomed, loved, and embraced at your church? Do you regularly have people who are without Christ showing up? Asking questions? Kicking the tires? If people far from God aren't coming to your church, you need to identify why. Some reasons could include:

- Your church members don't have relationships with the lost.
- Your people are too embarrassed to bring their friends to your church.
- Your building, your services, or the people in your church are subtly communicating, "Stay away."

Do whatever it takes to make your ministry a place that welcomes people who don't know Christ.

2. A Clear Explanation of the Gospel Story

Some churches preach a message that might be straight from the Bible and what some would call deep, but they assume that everyone who is listening is already a Christian. They teach the believer and forget that so many of their listeners have not yet crossed the line of faith. Others preach simply "how to have a better life" type messages. That may be helpful, but don't expect people to be saved. If messages contain more self-help than gospel, people will not hear and embrace the Good News.

When Jesus came to earth, he was full of both grace and truth. (See John 1:14.) That's why I like the idea of offering comfort and confrontation simultaneously. At the same moment, we welcome people with our comfortable environment and friendliness *and* confront them lovingly with truth. If people don't see themselves as sinners, they will never see their need for a savior. I suggest that you invite people to follow Christ every time you meet.

3. Genuine Faith

Finally, you need real faith. If you don't *really* believe in the power of Christ to change lives, people will know it. The opposite is true as well. If you believe with every fiber of your being that Christ can and will transform lives through the power of his grace, people will sense it, feel it, and often come to believe it as well.

So You Think You Have *It*

You may have read this chapter and thought, *I'm part of a very evangelistic ministry.* Thankfully, today we're witnessing many churches seeing dozens, hundreds, even thousands of people finding Christ. If that's you, I praise God with you. But here is a quick caution. Let's not boast in something that isn't ours to boast in. Ultimately, we preach, we pray, we invite, we believe, but we know it's Jesus who changes lives.

When we start to measure our success by God's performance, we're treading on dangerous ground. I try to take the viewpoint of the veteran rescue diver, played by Kevin Costner, in the 2006 movie *The Guardian*. At the end of the movie, the up-and-coming hotshot diver asks the retiring legendary diver, "What's your number?" He wants to know how many rescues the record holder carries. The young and competitive diver is assuming he'll hear maybe three hundred rescues.

Instead, Costner's character replies, "What's my number? My number is twenty-two."

The young guy is shocked. "Twenty-two," he says with great disappointment. "I thought you'd saved many more than that."

The veteran looks back over his shoulder and says, "Twenty-two is the number of people that I lost. That's the only number I ever counted."

Instead of boasting in how many people they've seen saved, those who have *it* realize how many more God wants to reach.

It Factors

- When we love deeply, love makes us do things we wouldn't otherwise do.
- To have *it*, we have to care about those who are far from God. Many people don't.
- We need to recognize that our friends desperately need Jesus.
- When our churches look inward instead of outward, we're basically saying to nonbelievers, "You can just go to hell."
- Outreach is a team event, and we each have a part to play.
- Be careful not to blame yourself if someone rejects Christ. If you do, you might be tempted to take credit when someone accepts him.
- Love overcomes any obstacle. We need to be willing to do whatever it takes to reach people who are far from God.
- We need to have the faith to clearly share the gospel story and expect people to respond.

Questions for Discussion or Reflection

1. Do you love people who don't know Christ? Do the leaders of your church? On a scale of one to ten (ten being the highest),

what is the evangelistic temperature of your church? Are you willing to lose some people from your church to reach those without Christ?

2. What are you doing to reach the lost? When is the last time you had a lost person in your home? What is the most recent spiritual conversation you had with a nonbeliever? Who are you praying for to receive Christ?

3. Is your church focused more outward or inward? Would a guest clearly understand the gospel after attending your church for one month? Would you bring a nonbeliever to your church every week? Why or why not? If you said no, discuss what needs to change.

4. A great evangelistic ministry should offer both comfort and confrontation. Is your ministry more comforting or confronting? What do you need to do better to offer a balance of grace and truth?

CHAPTER 10

Kingdom-Mindedness

What we have done for ourselves alone dies with us;
what we have done for others and the world remains
and is immortal.

—Albert Pike

A while back, I bumped into an older lady who recognized me as the pastor of Life.Church. She explained that she was a member of another church in town. Although I didn't know her pastor well, I said that I'd heard a lot of great things about him. She responded, "Wow! I can't believe you're speaking well of the competition." Shocked, I explained that in no way did I view her church as a competitor. She shot back, "Well, your church is definitely *our* competition. We're fighting to make sure we get as many members as we can before you and other churches get them all."

God's heart must break over that kind of attitude. Jesus said in Luke 11:17, "Any kingdom divided against itself will be ruined, and a house divided against itself will fall." Seventeenth-century Puritan minister Richard Baxter echoed Jesus' sentiment when he lamented, "Is it not enough that all the world is against us, but we must also be against one another? O happy days of persecution, which drove us together in love, whom the sunshine of liberty and prosperity crumbles into dust by our contentions!"

The more possessive and competitive we are, the more divided we become. Virtually every ministry I've ever known that had *it* was not divisive. The leaders were kingdom minded: our seventh *it* leadership ingredient.

What do I mean by kingdom minded?

A kingdom-minded ministry is one whose leaders care more about what God is doing everywhere than what God is doing right here. Kingdom-minded leaders know it's not just about their own ministry. A kingdom-minded ministry is generous and eager to partner with others to get more done for the glory of God.

It's hard to have *it* without desiring that other ministries succeed. When you have *it,* you know that it doesn't belong to you. It belongs to God. He gives it. And since it is his and not yours, you're grateful to have it and willing to share it.

Those who have *it* know it is not about them. It is not about their personal names. It is not about North Point, Elevation Church, Transformation Church, Gateway Church, Wesley United Methodist, First Baptist, First Presbyterian, First Christian, Calvary Chapel, Hope City, Redeemer Covenant, Fresh Life, Lord of Life Lutheran, Holy Ghost Temple of Righteous Praise, or whatever your church is called. *It* is not about *your* student ministry, *your* children's ministry, *your* YouTube presence, *your* church app, *your* new logo or website. And *it* is certainly not about your name. *It* is about Jesus. There's no other name under heaven by which we can be saved, and so no other name really matters. It's all about him.

Those who have *it* know it is not about them.

I learned this the hard way. There was one particular year in our church when we definitely didn't have *it*. This happened to be the year our church didn't grow. I think we didn't grow because we had lost focus—*I* had lost focus—and *it* blurred, faded, and disappeared.

One weekend that year, I was driving between our two campuses to speak. Each time I made that trip, I passed several churches. By the looks of one's empty parking lot, very few people were attending. With a combination of pride and pity, I prayed, *God, help this little church. I pray you would bless them and they'd reach a ton of new people.*

As I was praying, I felt like God asked me a question. *Craig, would you be excited if their growth exceeded yours?*

My honest answer was no.

That's hard to admit. No, I wouldn't have been happy if this church outgrew ours. It wasn't that I didn't want them reaching people. I just wanted to reach more. No matter how you slice that apple, I was territorial, insecure, and self-centered. While I had a heart for God's kingdom, my biggest desire was to build my kingdom, and God simply won't bless that. He *shouldn't.* I think that's why we weren't growing. If I were God, I wouldn't have grown our church either.

Napoleon Bonaparte once said, "I am surrounded by priests who repeat incessantly that their kingdom is not of this world and yet they lay their hands on everything they can get." Do you know any pastors like that? We say our church or ministry is not about us. But for many of us, "us" is all we can talk or think about. Not only is our kingdom not of this world but to build our kingdoms is surely one of the grossest sins. After I recognized my sinful attitude, my prayers changed. *God, make me more generous. Expand my heart for others. Make me a kingdom-minded leader.*

As pastors and Christian leaders, we should be thrilled when other ministries succeed. You may think you are, but have you noticed how much easier it is to be pumped for those who are growing in *another* town? *Yeah, God! I'm thrilled their ministry in that other state is growing!* But if they're in *my* town, it's easy to feel threatened or competitive. *What? The church down the street is doing well? They must be preaching a feel-good message.*

That attitude is wrong.

It's dangerous.

I'd go so far as to say that God won't let a ministry keep *it* for long if they won't give it away. Keeping it to yourself is a sure way to kill it. Ministries that don't have much of it often work hard to guard what little of it they have. What's funny about *it* is that the more you try to hoard it, the less of it you tend to have. The more you're willing to give it away, the more of it God seems to give.

I Was Willing to Take from Others, But . . .

Have you ever had one of those times when you were preparing a message, but God seemed to be playing the silent game?

It was a Saturday night sometime in the first year of our church, hours before I was supposed to preach, and I had nothing. I prayed, read my Bible, and prayed some more. Sometimes when I'm preparing, God empowers the process, almost like he's inspiring every word. Other times, it's like he doesn't even exist. This was one of those times.

Panic. Desperation. *God, where are you? Please give me something worthwhile to share. I promise I'll study better, be nicer to my wife, give more money, take that trip to Africa I've been avoiding, read the terms and conditions on my iPhone updates before agreeing to them.*

Then I did it. (For years I had heard of those who did it, but I'd never done it.) Well, I guess technically I didn't do it. I let someone else do it. I listened to a Rick Warren message, reworked it some, added my own illustrations, and preached it the next day. *Gasp.* To my surprise, God blessed it and used it. I suddenly learned to lean on those who had gone before me.

Back in the 1990s some of the better-known churches had tape ministries. (If you don't know what an overhead projector was, you might not remember cassette tapes either. These were popular after eight-tracks and before CDs.) I started ordering other pastors' tapes, and they helped me learn to preach. With little experience teaching God's Word, I was doomed to lay some eggs. (That means to preach some sucky sermons.) But seasoned preachers spoke into my life and into the lives of everyone who was attending Life.Church in its infancy. Most amazing, these pastors didn't even know. Certainly, their messages ministered to me, but that's not what I mean. I listened to these pastors, borrowed from them, made their messages my own, and after giving them credit, I preached "our" messages.

Then when I discovered Fellowship Church and North Point Church, Pastor Ed Young and Pastor Andy Stanley each opened my eyes to different ways to do ministry and communicate God's truth. Their insight taught me how to harness my renewed mind and how to be creative spiritually. I occasionally borrowed their titles, phrases, and points, and then used them at my church to reach more people than I could have on my own. (The only problem is I don't look as cool as Andy standing by his television, and I can't pull off Ed's edgy illustrations.)

Many of the great communicators invite other ministers to use their messages. During my early years of ministry, I benefited countless times from others' hard work. Standing on the shoulders of great communicators and leaders, while submitting to God's fresh direction, I was empowered by God to reach more people than I ever dreamed possible.

Then one day, I heard about a guy who preached one of *my* series. *The low-down, no-good, sermon-stealing preacher! How could he do that? That's my sermon!*

At first, I felt protective of my hard work. Then I remembered that I had done the same thing and that God had used what I learned from others to make an impact for him.

I was willing to take from others but initially hesitant to be generous with what I wrongly called mine. Finally, I realized I should be honored and thrilled that someone would compliment my work in such a way.

God quickly changed my heart from being defensive and territorial to being more kingdom minded. I was so pumped. What an honor! Did I *really* produce something someone else could use? Was it possible for other preachers to benefit from *my* studying, as I had benefited from theirs? I prayed, *God, please use me to help other pastors the way you've used other pastors to help me.*

If you're looking to find more of *it* in your ministry, maybe you should look for more ways to give whatever part of it you have to others. That's what I've been learning and becoming increasingly passionate about with each passing day.

Sharing *It*

Have you ever asked yourself what would happen if churches really worked together? Someone once said, "Snowflakes are one of nature's most fragile things, but just look at what they can do when they stick together." Think of what believers could do if we partnered together. Instead of being jealous, territorial, or easily threatened, what if we became extravagantly generous with our resources, ideas, and ministries? Do you think God would up your *it*? (When it comes to creative sermon titles, "Up Your It" just might be one.)

It finally hit me that while I grumbled and griped because so few people practice kingdom generosity, I never did anything about it. I was selfish. I wanted others to be generous and helpful, yet I wasn't. Then God's Spirit changed my heart.

Having learned from others, I wanted to pass along the wealth. As our church grew, more people asked for our ideas and support. One of the most common things churches asked was to use our videos, artwork, creative elements, and messages. As demand increased, we were tempted to sell our resources to increase revenue. More money means more ministry—there's certainly nothing wrong with that. Every church I know that sells their messages and creative content uses the profits to reach more people. They have massive organizations, with overhead and employees, providing valuable, affordable resources. More power to them.

Like other churches, we wanted to help other ministries around the world, but launching a division to do that didn't fit our vision. We prayed, *Lord, how can we partner with other ministries, without wasting your time and money, to advance your kingdom?*

Eventually God gave us a wild idea, one that was so crazy it just might work. What if, we asked idealistically, we just gave away our creative content? We had some hard discussions. We knew building the systems, supporting the bandwidth, raising up the staff, and managing the site would cost us something, but God was clearly calling us to take this leap of faith, and the investment would be minuscule compared with the potential spiritual dividends. Life. Church Open Network was born.

Some of our team members worried that if we gave away our stuff, we might lose *it*. If someone else had some of what we consider special, wouldn't that diminish our impact? We quickly discovered the opposite is true. The more we gave away, the more God used the same resources in other places, and instead of depleting our creative ideas, we discovered more. The more of *it* we gave away, the more of it God gave back. Isn't that exactly what Jesus promised? In Luke 6:38, Jesus says, "Give, and it will be given to you. A good measure, pressed down, shaken together and running over, will be poured into your lap. For with the measure you use, it will be measured to you."

A self-centered and competitive ministry generally loses *it*. A kingdom-minded ministry seems to attract it. "Give, and *it* will be given to you." As you become more generous, God likely will increase your impact and reach. As your influence expands, you likely will attract stronger leaders, pastors, and creative ministers.

As your library of ministry resources grows, you could sell what you have with integrity. That might be the right way for you to go. With the proceeds, you could dig water wells for the thirsty, build homes for orphans, pay for your television outreach, or plant churches.

A kingdom-minded ministry seems to attract it.

But you might consider something completely different, more possible now than ever because of technology. You could take what you've created, spend just a little more, and make it available to others. What if you gave as much of *it* away as possible?

If you choose to share *it,* here's what I believe will happen:

- *You'll help pastors do better ministry.* It's thrilling. Pastors from around the world, in churches of every size, have contacted us to say they're benefiting from what we've already created. In the first month after we launched Life.Church Open, with no advertising whatsoever, more than one thousand churches in eleven countries downloaded more than ten thousand pieces from the site. Today, the number of resources that have helped other ministries is in the hundreds of millions.

- *You'll develop kingdom partnerships.* We're making friends with leaders we wouldn't have met otherwise. Our friendships have grown beyond our expectations, and we're working together to find staff, share ideas, and even partner to plant new campuses and churches.

- *You'll model effective stewardship.* You'll extend the life of your creative material. If you preach a sermon once, it's used once. If you give it away, it might be used fifty times. If five hundred people attend your church, and you spend five hundred dollars on staff and the use of equipment to make a video, that video's cost is one dollar per person. But if just ten other churches use that same video, and each has 150 members, then you've dramatically reduced the cost to just twenty-five cents per person. Any pastor will tell you that God honors that kind of sensible faithfulness.

- *You'll encourage others to practice radical generosity.* Almost immediately after we launched Life.Church Open, several other churches followed suit. How cool is that?
- *God will bless you with more of it.* It might be more creative, biblical content and ideas. It could be generous givers or evangelistic leaders. God might send you more people who don't know Christ. The bottom line is that when you give *it,* God gives it back to you. As we've shared the ideas God has shared with us, he has sparked even more. Who's more creative than the Creator?
- *When you share* it, *kingdom unity emerges.* The things that divide us become less important. We all share our humanity, our fallenness. When we see others being real about who they are, we are drawn together and more likely to help each other. We also all share a mission, and sharing our resources wars against the competition mindset that breaks God's heart.
- *Really, you can't imagine what will happen.* Only God can see the whole picture. Just as a certain message, a certain song, or a certain turn of phrase can surprise you by catalyzing change in people, we often don't know what God's trying to do until we take a risk. If we truly believe we are his people, that this is his world, and we trust in him for eternity, what do we really have to lose?

You might think, *Well, it's easy to give a lot away when you are a big church with a lot of resources.* That might be true. But I believe God wants us to give *before* it's easy. That's when it takes faith. We started talking about giving our resources away during the toughest financial season in the history of our church. We had borrowed quite a bit of money and hit the peak of our debt (well over 23 million dollars). We knew that selling resources with integrity could be an income generator. But God called us to trust him by faith.

Along the way, we developed our Church Online Platform. We created it so we could do church online, but then realized it would benefit other churches. We knew we could sell it to generate income, but we decided to give it away. Pre-COVID, three thousand churches were using our Church Online Platform weekly. During the pandemic and time of quarantine, that number surged to more than twenty-five thousand churches. Our cost for providing our online platform jumped to more than $500,000 a month. That's a lot of money, but it's an honor because it's a kingdom-minded way we get to bless the church.

When we created the YouVersion Bible App, all the experts told us to run ads or sell the app for ninety-nine cents. But I came to faith because someone handed me a free Gideon's Bible. We want to give out free Bibles. The YouVersion Bible App is a contribution we can make to the body of Christ. And yeah, we could increase our resources if we sold it for ninety-nine cents. We're now well over half a billion installs—that would be a lot of income! But God has called us to trust him by faith.

I've always heard preachers say, "You can't outgive God." God proved that true. The very weekend we announced our decision to serve other churches with free resources, our offerings "mysteriously" jumped considerably. It wasn't just one week; they didn't drop. It was only a matter of time before we started chipping away at our loans and, by the grace of God, became debt free just a few years later. I'm convinced God honored our decision to bless other churches. If you take a step of faith with kingdom-minded generosity, I know you will bless others, and I pray God will surprise you with blessings greater than you can imagine.

John Wesley said it well: "Do all the good you can. By all the means you can, in all the ways you can, in all the places you can, at all the times you can, to all the people you can, as long as you ever can." Churches with *it* model that. They know we can do far more together than we can apart.

Other Ways to Share *It*

Whenever God blesses your ministry, I pray you'll be hungry to partner with others. Whatever he gives you, share it. Ask yourself what you can give away. Here are some ideas for becoming more kingdom minded.

I know several churches that share buildings. If you have a building or even a room that goes unused, maybe you could offer the use of your facility free to a church plant or an international church that meets when you're not using it. Perhaps the church plant might buy you a new sound system or video projector in exchange for using your building. With careful planning and good communication, everyone wins.

How about taking up an offering for another ministry? Suppose another church in your town undertakes a building project. Receive an offering and send it to them. Your church can model kingdom generosity and help the family of Christ.

As a kingdom-minded church, what if you prayed for another church in your city each Sunday that you gathered for worship? Imagine the power of prayer touching God's heart as you ask him to bless, strengthen, and provide for other churches to fulfill their mission and glorify God. Think about how it would inspire your church to cheer on others and celebrate their ministry as you each impact your city in different ways.

You can also commit to speak well of other ministries. To embrace others, you have to acknowledge that your way of doing ministry is not the only way, or even the best way. If everyone did ministry the way you do, we'd never reach the world. You can decide never to talk badly about another Christian leader or church. Work to brag on other ministries, especially in your own community.

I try to encourage pastors not to "push off" other ministries. I'm guessing that many spiritual leaders may not even recognize they are subtly making others look bad when they say things like, "Most pastors won't tell you this, but I will tell you the truth." (Translation: I'm better than other pastors.) "Some churches water it down, but at our church we preach the uncompromised Word of God." (Translation: Our church is better than others.) Rather than saying what you are not, just say what you are. Be confident in your calling without making others look bad or less than.

You may also think about ways to partner with other churches and ministries. Well over three hundred thousand American churches are trying to do separate missions work. What if you partnered with another church (or two or twenty) to make a difference in one significant place? It just might end the days when you find yourself canceling missions trips because of a lack of interest. Instead, your trips will overflow with participants and you might have to book more.

Perhaps your church can't afford a full-time singles pastor. Consider bringing four or five churches together for monthly singles events. All the churches can still minister to their single adults and maybe reach some new people. Some of the singles might even thank you when they find godly wives or husbands. (Or write you bitter emails if they don't.)

As God gives it to you, give it away. (If it helps to motivate you, sing the lyrics of the old Red Hot Chili Peppers song "Give It Away," which says, "Give it away, give it away, give it away now" over and over and over again.)

Remember where you find *it*? You find it in people! One of the most generous gifts you can give is the gift of people. You might prayerfully send individuals or families with spiritual gifts, or just wonderful hearts, to other churches. Several times at Life.Church, I've promoted other churches. In all of the communities where we meet, we make a list of other healthy churches and tell our attenders, "If you aren't making a difference or growing spiritually at Life.Church, try one of these." Then we describe some of the strengths of each one. Many people take us up on that challenge and later write us thank-you notes. We cleared some needed seats to reach more people, and other churches in town were grateful and stronger.

As God gives *it* to you, give it away.

We have even been honored by several churches who've called and said in effect, "We don't have *it*, but we want it. Can we merge ministries?" We've partnered with a few churches that decided to become a part of Life.Church. Across the country, many ministries are realizing they can do more united than they can divided.

Be generous with *it*! Find a church that could benefit from what you're doing and adopt them. What would that look like? I'm not sure. You prayerfully decide. How can you help? Perhaps your leaders can mentor theirs. Maybe you can give them your old choir robes or your church van. You might help them find the worship leader they're looking for. Whatever you can do, do it.

As church leaders, we should continually ask, "What do we have that could benefit the kingdom?" I promise you that God has given you something valuable.

It could be your:

- time
- ideas
- people
- talent

- buildings
- reputation
- finances
- blog
- extra worship leaders

Remember the lady I told you about at the beginning of the chapter? The one who said our church was her church's competition? I bumped into her again several months later. She approached me humbly and said, "I think I owe you an apology." She explained how her pastor was using some of our resources and how excited he was to partner with us to reach people. She smiled from ear to ear and hugged me, fighting back tears as she said, "Thank God we're on the same team."

Whatever you have, remember it is not yours. It belongs to God and he wants you to give it away. Then watch as God stretches it, multiplies it, and spreads it around!

What can you do? More than you think.

It Factors

- The more possessive and competitive we are, the more divided we become.
- A kingdom-minded ministry is more about what God is doing everywhere than what God is doing right here.
- If you are kingdom minded, you will speak well of and promote other churches and ministries.
- A kingdom-minded ministry is generous and hungry to partner with others to get more done for the glory of God.
- When you have *it*, you know that it doesn't belong to you. It belongs to God. He gives it. Since it is his and not yours, you're willing to share it.

- The more you try to keep *it*, the less of it you tend to have. The more you are willing to give it away, the more of it God seems to give.
- Kingdom-minded churches ask, "What do we have that we can give away?" and, "How can we partner with other ministries to grow God's kingdom?"

Questions for Discussion or Reflection

1. Do you see other ministries as teammates or as competitors? When a new church or a similar ministry starts close to you, do you feel excited or threatened? Why? What can you do to train your mind to be focused on the kingdom rather than focused inward?

2. Would you be thrilled if God blessed a smaller ministry down the road more than he is blessing yours? Why or why not?

3. Is your leadership focused more on building your ministry or on building God's kingdom? What can you do as leaders to become more kingdom minded? What can you do to help other churches? What do you have that you could give to another ministry? How can you promote kingdom unity with your words?

4. British evangelist, pastor, and author Alan Redpath said, "Before we can pray, 'Lord, Thy kingdom come,' we must be willing to pray, 'My kingdom go.'" How do you think God wants to expand his kingdom through you? Is there any part of your ministry that is more your kingdom than God's kingdom? What in your heart or actions needs to change?

PART 3

WHAT IT MEANS TO GET *IT* BACK AND GUARD IT

I am no master chef, but I do try to cook from time to time. When I do, I need to use a recipe because I don't have the spiritual gift of cheffing. (Is there a spiritual gift of cheffing? Is cheffing even a word?)

You've probably used a recipe or two, and so you know the magic ingredient in a recipe is . . . the ingredients. I told you about the surprising ingredients in my wife's amazing spaghetti sauce.

The ingredients come together to develop the flavors and create the dish. They are so important some chefs won't reveal them. If you've watched a TV show where a chef in a famous restaurant shares how they make their specialty, you know they often will hold back from telling you all the ingredients.

We have just gone through the seven "ingredients" that contribute to a church's having *it*. I've held nothing back. I believe if your ministry has those ingredients, you will have *it*.

But it's not *just* the ingredients.

If you gave me just a list of ingredients, as a *very* amateur cook I would give you a panicked look. I now know what I need, but I don't know what to do with them!

- Am I baking these ingredients? Or grilling them?
- Do I put the butter in the pan, and then cook the steak in the butter? Or do I cook the steak and then add the butter?
- Do I cut up the carrots and, if so, how do I cut the carrots—into big chunks or julienned? (Confession: I don't even know what *julienned* means.)
- Do I put the fresh basil in the sauce right from the start, or add it at the end?

In a similar way, we have seven ingredients that together create *it*. But what do you do with them? How do you apply them? How do you lead, on a daily basis, like *it* matters?

That's what we're going to walk through next. Three ways to lead like *it* matters:

1. Mindset over model
2. Creating systems that empower *it*
3. Centered around *it*

So if you're ready, let's learn how to make a soufflé. (Or macaroni and cheese.) (Or a chimichanga.) (I don't know—whatever dish you think represents *it!*)

CHAPTER 11

Mindset over Model

Once your mindset changes, everything on the outside will change along with it.
—Steve Maraboli

I have never been accused of being a stylish dresser. If you've seen me and thought I had some fashion sense, it's probably because I had help.

One issue is that I am colorblind. There is a brand of clothes for children called Garanimals. Each article of clothing has a different animal on the label. You know a shirt matches a pair of pants if the animals on each go together. When I was a kid, Garanimals were my only hope for not looking stupid.

In college, I didn't have the money to keep up with the changing styles. What I did have was T-shirts. Being a college tennis player (free team shirts) and in a fraternity (themed shirts for every party and event) meant I had tons of T-shirts. In the winter, it was too cold for T-shirts, so I was in trouble. That's when three buddies and I decided to start a style trend. We agreed to wear T-shirts (for the cool factor) over sweatshirts (for the warmth factor). I am sad to report that style never caught on.

Today, I may give you the impression I have decent fashion sense. Nope. I need help. No, I don't wear Garanimals (though an adult version of Garanimals might be a million dollar idea!), but I do get help, lots of help. On my own, I just can't figure out the right style.

So a church realizes they don't have *it*. They decide it's time to get it. They're ready to do whatever it takes.

What happens next?

Too often they think they need to change the style of their church. The leaders of a struggling traditional church might conclude, "We need to start a contemporary service to reach young people." Soon they're looking for a worship leader with tattoos and cool jeans. They buy some drums. They put up a sign outside that says "Traditional Service at 9:45 and Contemporary Service at 11:15." Problem solved, right?

Not even close. Why? Because the problem is not the style of the church.

It's not the model; it's the mindset.

We've walked through seven leadership ingre-
dients that lead to *it*. But what do you do with them? How do you apply them? As you grow in each of those seven It Factors, how do you think about *it*

It's not the model; it's the mindset.

and lead toward *it*? We're going to do a deep dive into three ideas that will help. The first is mindset over model.

To understand how the mindset needs to change, let's start with how church models have evolved over the past few decades. (I'm talking primarily of churches in the West. I know there are broader and different examples globally.) Let's think back to the 1950s. During the *Happy Days* era of churches, it was normal for American families to attend Sunday service together. During this time, most church buildings looked similar. Many were attractive, ornate, displaying stained-glass windows and featuring tall steeples. Most churches were long and narrow with wooden seats called pews. When people worshiped, they sang hymns to an organ accompaniment. People loved it. Until they didn't.

As values and interests slowly and subtly shifted, a newer generation started attending church less. It wasn't that they didn't need God, they just didn't see a need for church. Church didn't seem necessary or relevant. They went less frequently. Then on Easter and Christmas only. Then some stopped going altogether.

Enter the renegade spiritual leaders of the 1980s. With an undying loyalty to the church and an aching love for the lost, some young, revolutionary (and harshly criticized) pastors blazed new spiritual trails. Their mantra was clear. "We never change the message. But our methods must change." And change they did! They stopped insisting that real Christian men wear suits and godly women wear dresses to worship. They changed the standards almost overnight. These new churches screamed, "Come as you are! Everyone is welcome!" For the first time, some people wore blue jeans to church. *Gasp!* It got wilder from there. Some wore tennis shoes. *Double gasp!* In one church, there was even a guy spotted wearing a baseball cap! Hard to believe, but it's true.

I grew up wearing an uncomfortable suit to church. (No, they didn't have Garanimal suits.) Honestly, I hated going to church. I didn't hate God. Quite the opposite. I knew I needed God. I wanted God. I just couldn't seem to find him in church. During the one-hour service on Sunday, I always felt a sick combination of bored and confused. But with the rise of "contemporary church," everything changed. Rather than hard, uncomfortable pews, churches had soft, comfortable chairs. They stopped singing from a book and started viewing the lyrics on a screen. Instead of worshiping with an organ, churches worshiped with a band. To the early adopters, these changes were born of an authentic desire to engage the lost. Church could be relevant, engaging, and fun.

The new model seemed to work. Some of these contemporary

churches grew. Since other pastors wanted to learn, these successful churches hosted conferences. Other pastors emulated their model.

Is that a problem? Well, maybe. Because remember, it's not the model. It's the mindset.

Pastors who started a different way of doing church did it because they cared about people who were without Christ. They believed wholeheartedly in the transformational power of the gospel. They just thought the older method of delivery was tired, outdated, and irrelevant. Their new model reflected their mindset of taking the gospel into a lost and broken world.

That works. That's *it*.

But I think somewhere along the way, some churches lost the mindset and instead trusted the model.

Now we find ourselves a couple of decades into the 2000s, and what was new and different thirty or forty years ago is mostly normal. Most newer church buildings look the same. Rather than having an altar, they have a stage. Instead of having a solemn atmosphere, the worship service feels like a rock concert. The lobbies are bigger and full of free refreshments. If the church can afford it, the kids' room rivals Disney. (And, yes, I am aware that I could be describing my own church.)

The problem is that the power is not in the model. I am even beginning to wonder whether the model we've been using is tired.

I'll bet you don't know many people who are excited about the contemporary church model. When is the last time you heard someone say, "Wow! Let's go to that new church. I hear they have dramas there!" Or, "Is it true? My friend told me you can wear shorts to that church in the summer. That's so crazy!" You won't hear someone at the grocery store celebrating, "Dude, they've got drums in the church. It's totally rad." The new style isn't new anymore. It's not different. It's almost expected. I might even suggest that contemporary is the new traditional.

It may be time for the style of church to change again. If so, that would be fine. In one important sense, it really wouldn't matter at all. Because the model never changes lives. Jesus changes lives. *It* is never about the model. It comes from a faith-driven mindset of reaching people who are without Christ.

That's why we don't need to obsess about the model. We need to obsess about the mindset.

New Generation, New Thinking

In their book, *Growing Young,* Kara Powell, Jake Mulder, and Brad Griffin make compelling arguments about today's younger generation and how church leaders should approach them. (Many of my ideas in this chapter are derived from their book.) They explain how the younger generation feels more alone, more stressed, and more afraid than most of us can imagine. Those feelings were only exacerbated when they spent months locked up in their homes fearing a global pandemic. They are exposed to the world's suffering in their daily feeds. They have watched the injustices of brutal mistreatment streamed directly to their mobile devices for as long as they can remember. This emerging generation doesn't know a world without social media, the drug that sells the illusion of intimacy but leaves us drowning in comparisons and craving real connection. They are bombarded with the daily temptation of porn, which isolates, shames, and redefines how they relate. Most teens or twentysomethings fear they won't have what it takes to make it in life. They are asking questions of purpose and meaning. "Why am I here? Where do I belong? Do I have what it takes?"

It's not that the emerging generation isn't spiritual. Many people are. But there is a big difference between being spiritual and knowing Christ. Some would say the dominant belief of the emerging generation is moralistic therapeutic deism (a term introduced in the book *Soul Searching* in 2005). What in the world is that, you ask? It's simpler than it sounds.

1. Moralism equates religion with being a good, moral person.
2. Therapeutic equates faith to feeling better about oneself.
3. Deism is a belief that God exists, but he's not involved in people's daily affairs.[8]

Many in the younger generation (and some in all generations) essentially believe that you are supposed to be nice and, if you are, a mostly uninvolved God will make your life better.

Can you see the challenges this mindset creates? Sin isn't in the equation. It implies that happiness is the goal. Therefore, if something makes you happy, it must be good. If it doesn't make you happy, it must be bad. Happiness, not truth, is the ultimate arbiter. If God doesn't make your life better, he isn't doing his job. This teaching is not the gospel and in many ways is its opposite.

I saw this belief when talking to a young guy from church I'll call Grant. Grant grew up in our church, was baptized in his early teens, and attends church faithfully. He started telling me that one of his student leaders was encouraging him to stop looking at porn. Grant seemed frustrated and even confused by his youth leader's challenge to fight for sexual purity in his mind. Grant explained passionately, "I know I've even heard you preach about porn being wrong and dangerous, and I'm sure that was true when you were growing up. But ya gotta admit things have changed. You can't expect a guy not to look occasionally, can you?" What's most interesting to me is that Grant, who is very involved in the life of the church, believes something could have been wrong before but is not wrong today.

Grant's view is rooted in moralistic therapeutic deism, not historic Christianity with its concepts of sin, repentance, and holiness.

This is why we as church leaders need not only to acknowledge this growing mindset but also to understand how and why a generation can rapidly drift from or reject historic Christian roots. When we seek to understand and empathize rather than condemn and judge, we can learn how to contextualize the unchanging message of the gospel to ever-changing cultural mindsets.

Warmth Is the New Cool

When it comes to church, so many of the younger generation are skeptical, jaded, and distrusting. I'm not saying I blame them. If I grew up seeing what they have seen, I'd likely have similar views. To reach them, we have to understand them. If we can't really understand them, we must at least empathize with them and truly care for them.

I promise they aren't looking for a certain style of church. While many pastors strive to make their ministries more relevant, a generation is rejecting "relevant" and crying out for "real." So many churches try to be slick, professional, hip, or cool, but they are hurting their chances with people who are not looking for cool, who just want someone who cares. To reach a younger generation, we must understand that relational warmth is the new cool.

> This generation is rejecting "relevant" and crying out for "real."

As the old quote goes, "People don't care how much you know until they know how much you care." Will you love them if they are different? Will you accept them even if they don't believe like you believe? Will you allow them to ask honest questions without making them feel stupid or less than? Will you love them even if you disagree?

It's not about the model. It's about the mindset.

Let's talk straight. It's easy for pastors to get caught up in the numbers. Most of us want to reach more people. I sincerely hope you do. But hurting people don't care about the size of our churches.

They are wondering about the size of our hearts. They are not looking for a church that cares about numbers. They crave a community
that cares about people.

Three Essential Mindsets

If *it* is all about mindset, what should our minds be set on? Let's
focus on three essential mindsets.

1. We Must Be People Focused and Jesus Centered

"People focused and Jesus centered? Wow, Craig, that's crazy! No
one has ever proposed such a radical idea." I know, I know, we all
believe in being people focused and Jesus centered. But we don't
always show it in our actions. If it's about mindset, we will truly
embrace and practically live out the idea: People are our hearts.
Jesus is our message.

Those two sentences matter. *People are our hearts.* In other
words, we *really* care. People aren't a number to grow our church.
They aren't projects for us to help. They are children of God, people
we are called and compelled to love.

We don't stop there. *Jesus is our message.* Our message isn't how
to be happy or to get out of debt or to have a better marriage or to
grow in expositional understanding of the book of Revelation. Our
message is Jesus. Again, I assume you would agree. But we need to be
more Jesus centered, Jesus focused, and Jesus driven than ever before.
In a culture that disapproves of formal religion, dislikes power, and
is distrusting of authority, we must point people to Jesus.

Even if someone is spiritual, it's a big leap for them to believe in a
God they can't see. To some people, the idea of the Holy Spirit might
seem unusual at best and creepy at worst. Jesus, however, is not only
the answer, he's also easier to explain and difficult not to like.

Jesus is a real historical person. Almost no one debates that. So we're off to a solid start. And even if you aren't religious at all, what Jesus taught is beautiful.

- Love God.
- Love one another.
- The greatest is the one who serves.
- With God, all things are possible.
- I have come not to be served but to serve.
- Lay down your life.
- My peace I give to you.
- Come to me and I will give you rest.

Jesus loved outcasts. He befriended sinners. He embraced the broken. He defended the weak. He stood for justice. He healed the sick. He never sinned. He suffered unjustly. He died for our sins. You don't have to be religious, spiritual, or a church member to appreciate what Jesus taught and how he lived.

To reach people, we don't just preach Jesus, we follow Jesus—not just in our words but in how we live. We are not just teaching what we believe, we are showing people how to live and love like Jesus. Moralistic therapeutic deism implies that God wants you to be nice, and if you are, he will make your life better. The Jesus-centered gospel says, "You've sinned, but Jesus restores, frees, liberates, redeems, and makes you new. It's by his grace that you are saved." Our message isn't to join a church but to belong to Christ. It's not to behave like us but to believe in Jesus. (I'm not discounting personal holiness, but holiness starts with the work of God, not with our effort.)

To have *it*, we must be all about Jesus.

2. We Must Allow for In-Process Conversions

As we are sharing Jesus, we also want to grow in patience for God's work in other people. Instead of expecting people who come to our church to behave like mature believers, we are wise to allow for "in-process conversions." We don't find that term in the Bible, but we see examples of it all through the Scriptures.

Most of us celebrate immediate conversions. You know the dramatic "I was blind, but now I see" stories. The party guy gets saved (like me). The drug addict prays to Jesus and never does drugs again. The overbearing husband experiences the grace of Jesus and becomes new. We love big life-changing moments like Saul's, who was saved on the road to Damascus. One minute he is killing Christians. Shortly after, he's risking his life preaching about Jesus.

Some people will be transformed in a moment. But for many, conversion takes time, maybe even a lot of time. It might be the girl who was sexually abused for years. She comes to church, but her trust is low. She steps toward the things of Jesus, then quickly retreats. Months later, she comes back to church and appears to be more open. But she's hesitant and finds it hard to trust. Who could blame her? Or perhaps it's the business guy whose wife drags him to church. He's driven, successful, and on top of his game with his business on the rise. He doesn't see much need for God. His life is good. Then one week at church, he's impacted by a song. In the moment, he is open to the Spirit's work. But the mood fades and he's back to his normal. Months later, he loses a big deal and a friend prays for him. Again, he's open, but not for long. These people are "in process." They are spiritually open, even occasionally curious or hungry. Then they are hesitant. But they might be open again soon.

To have *it,* you need to accept that the journey to Christ may take longer today for many people than it did in years past. People have questions. Many have way more complicated questions. They don't want bumper-sticker answers. When a person doubts God because they lost a baby, they don't want an easy Christian answer like, "The Bible says it. I believe it. That settles it."

We need to give people permission to doubt on their journey toward faith. Thomas doubted and Jesus didn't reject him. When someone is struggling and asking real faith questions, we can enter the struggle with them. We don't need to have all the answers. It's probably even good when we occasionally don't. Instead of trying to solve someone's problems, sometimes we should just hurt with them. We can have honest conversations. Let people ask the hard questions. Listen. Empathize. And continue to trust the Spirit of God to do what we cannot.

Instead of being angry when someone goes back to drugs or doubts the Bible or gives in to their sexual addiction, we can believe this might be part of the process. Think about Peter. When did he get saved? When was he mature in his faith? He left his boat and career to follow Jesus. Then he tried to talk Jesus out of his mission and had Jesus call him the devil. He declared his loyalty to Jesus, then denied him multiple times. Peter preached boldly at Pentecost, then Paul had to confront him because he snubbed the gentiles. It seems Peter was constantly a story in process. We need to have the same patience with people that God had with Peter.

3. We Should Obsess over Giving Keys and Tees

In today's culture, churches that have *it* obsess over giving keys and tees. (Stick with me. I promise this will make sense.)

To illustrate, let's take two imaginary churches. We will call one Local Mega Church (LMC) and the other Small Faithful Bible Church (SFBC). LMC and SFBC are two miles away from each other. LMC is the talk of the town. They have five services at this location, which is only one of three campuses in the city. SFBC is small, but strong. Even though just 120 attend SFBC, they are involved in the church and love Jesus.

Why do you think people stay at SFBC even though LMC is just down the road? Two main reasons. People tend to stay at SFBC because they are needed and because they are known. With only 120 people, each person has a job, a role, a ministry position. Someone unlocks the church, someone else greets, there's a person who fills the communion cups, another visits the shut-ins, and someone makes meals for the sick. Everyone is needed. And everyone is known. Since the church is smaller, if anyone misses a service, everyone notices. By 2:00 p.m. on Sunday, the missing attender might get two texts and one call from friends making sure they are good.

Now let's take the booming church down the street. Why do people go to LMC? Honestly, there are too many reasons to list. The church is on fire. The worship leader is world class. The preaching may be the best in town (or at least the most energetic). The kids' ministry is a blast. The missions program is making a massive difference around the world. They have a sports ministry, a singles ministry, a divorce-care ministry, a get-out-of-debt ministry, a prep-for-marriage ministry, a how-to-lead-people-to-Christ ministry, a best-fashion-choices-for-the-colorblind ministry. (Okay, no church has that, but they should!) LMC has it all. Why do people attend the megachurch? Lots and lots of reasons.

But why do you think people leave LMC? Because the truth about LMC is that even though many people get saved there, lots still leave. It has a revolving door. There are two main reasons people don't stick. People tend to leave LMC because they are not needed and because they are not known. When someone comes to LMC, they notice everything is done with excellence. It seems like all the bases are covered. They don't feel like they can contribute. And since there are so many people at LMC, if you miss a week (or two or three or five months), it's not likely anyone will notice. They don't feel needed and they don't feel known. That's why to have *it*, you will want to give out keys and tees.

KEYS

All six of my kids are driving now. And yes, when each one turned sixteen, we doubled the amount of prayers we prayed. The most dramatic new-driver moment was with my oldest son, Sam. He had just passed his driving test and earned the money to pay for half of his car, as we had agreed. We were walking slowly together toward his car and the gravity of the moment set in. I told him soberly, "Sam, you have proven to be responsible. You worked hard. You saved your money. You passed your driver's test. And you are ready to drive." When my eyes met his, I could tell he felt prouder than I realized he might. He was emotional, and it got me emotional. "You are a young man now," I said as he took in the moment. "I trust you. Here are the keys." Sam smiled softly, took a big breath, and said, "Well, that's a lot of responsibility." Then he gave me a giant father-son hug.

Sam felt trusted, empowered, and responsible. Churches that have *it* help followers of Christ feel the same. They don't just go to church. They *are* the church, the embodiment of Christ on earth. Part of our responsibility as church leaders is to help people who are part of our churches to embrace their kingdom calling, their divine responsibility to represent Jesus. We need to let them know that they are needed.

That's one reason why our people-focused, Jesus-centered message should be clear and compelling. God doesn't just save us to give us a better life. He saves us so we can glorify him and serve people with our lives. We aren't just saved *from,* we are saved *for.* Yes, we are saved from our past sins. But we are saved for a future purpose. When Peter confessed the lordship of Christ, Jesus told him, "I will give you the *keys of the kingdom* of heaven" (Matt. 16:19a, emphasis mine). Jesus gave Peter the keys. Jesus told him, "Whatever you bind on earth will be bound in heaven, and whatever you loose on earth will be loosed in heaven" (v. 19b). Essentially Jesus said, "I trust you. I need you on my team."

> We aren't just saved *from,* we are saved *for.*

Churches that have *it* are churches that empower people to live *it.* Our message is not just "you are a sinner, so change." We help people see they are needed. God created them to be an important part of a larger community loving and impacting the world. Our language matters. That's why at Life.Church we don't just call people volunteers. We remind them they are volunteer spiritual leaders. Over and over again, we remind our staff that "we don't recruit volunteers, we release leaders. Volunteers do good things; leaders change the world." We are not just asking people to serve. We are empowering them to lead. We want them to know they are needed.

We also want them to be known.

TEES

My boys love soccer. Since we have satellite TV, they don't just watch pro teams from the United States, they have access to watch some of the greatest teams in the world, including Barcelona. I don't have enough knowledge to tell you whether "Barça" is truly the greatest team in the world. But to my boys, it's an indisputable fact. So what do you think they wear? Barça socks, Barça caps, and (most important) Barça T-shirts. They have never been to Spain and will never play professional soccer, but they proudly sport the jersey. One time, I asked them if they felt more important wearing the Barça team jersey. They both looked at me like I had just asked them the dumbest question in the world. Of course they felt important. The jersey revealed their loyalty.

At our church, we give away lots of Life.Church T-shirts. It wasn't a strategy at first. It started as an inexpensive way to appreciate people. But once a lot of people started having a lot of shirts, we noticed something happening around town. When a Life.Church person was wearing a Life.Church shirt and saw someone else wearing a Life.Church shirt, there was an immediate bond. "You're a part of my church? I love it there. I got saved three years ago!" Two people who had never met instantly belonged.

Churches that have *it* help people know they can belong even before they believe. Yep, that's right. Because we know becoming a disciple of Jesus can be a process, we show unconditional love. Just like I was nervous approaching the doors of the huge historic church, most everyone feels self-conscious or uncomfortable the first time they visit a church. And that's if they're already a Christian. If they are not, they are likely to be scared out of their minds. That's where love comes in. We want everything about our building, our services, and our people to communicate, "We were expecting you. You are welcome. You don't have to believe what we believe. You don't have to behave like we behave. This is a safe place to belong before you believe."

How will they get that sense of belonging? Let's start with how they won't. They won't feel like they are a part of your community because your worship team did a really cool secular walk-in song. They won't feel loved by the free donuts or the brilliant sermon illustrations or the new and overpriced LED wall you just knew would make the church double in size. Jesus said it best. (Doesn't he always?) He explained that they will know that we belong to him, that we are his disciples, *if* we love one another. (See John 13:35.)

Recently, I met a man at our church named Ali, who explained that he loves coming every week even though he's a Muslim. I asked him about his family, his background, and his personal interests. After several minutes of an engaging conversation, I politely asked why he loves our church when he has a different faith background. Ali smiled and said, "I had heard all the different ways Life.Church serves people in the city, and so I thought I'd come and help out. I started serving, and the people were so loving to me that I just kept on coming back." Ali hasn't changed his beliefs at this point, but he says he is loving learning about Jesus.

Churches that have *it* tend to love more people than churches that don't have *it*. But they don't just love the crowds. They love each and every person. Everyone matters to God, so everyone matters to us. Jesus told us that when a shepherd has one hundred sheep and one wanders off, the good shepherd leaves the ninety-nine to pursue the one. Do you have a heart for the one? Does your church have room for an Ali? Or a doubter? Or someone who is sexually confused? Or looks different?

Pastors and church leaders may want to grow their churches big and fast. That's a good place to start. But you won't grow *it* with the model. It's the mindset. The best way to grow a church is one by one. Jesus explained, "There is rejoicing in the presence of the angels of God over one sinner who repents" (Luke 15:10).

When Jesus told Peter he entrusted him with the keys to the kingdom, Jesus said, "I will build my church, and the gates of Hades will not overcome it" (Matt. 16:18). I try to remind myself that Jesus loves our church more than I do and that he is the one who builds it. How? He builds it through people. Jesus told us to preach the gospel. It's easy to lose our focus. The devil loves to distract us from the mission. Instead of being people focused and Jesus centered, we can start to think church is about us and our preferences. Rather than allowing for in-process conversions, having patience as the Spirit does what only he can do, we can slip into judgmentalism and pride, looking down on people who are not like us. We can also forget the power of helping people in the kingdom of God embrace that they are both needed and known.

The power isn't in a style of worship. State-of-the-art buildings don't change lives. Relevant sermon series are not the secret to church growth. It's never about a model. It's about a mindset, thinking like Jesus, embracing his mission, and showing his love.

Jesus didn't come for the healthy. He came for the sick.

It Factors

- Churches without *it* often think the solution is changing their church's style. It's not. The issue is not the model; it's the mindset.

- Throughout history, renegade church leaders have (sometimes dramatically) shifted the model and seen results. But the results have come because of the mindset that drove the change more than the new model.
- The church must be people focused and Jesus centered. Most Christians would say they are. We need to live it out in our actions and in our teaching.
- The church must allow for in-process conversions. We know that transformation is a process, and so we give people room to doubt and ask their questions.
- Instead of being angry when someone is slow in making spiritual progress or takes a step backward, we choose to believe this might be part of the process.
- We need to have the same patience with people that God has with us.
- We need to help people know they are needed and known.

Questions for Discussion or Reflection

1. Looking back at your history in ministry or at your church's history, where can you see a trust in models instead of mindset?

2. How have you seen moralistic therapeutic deism be an issue in the lives of Christ followers?

3. Are you and your church people focused? Where do you see people being viewed more as numbers or burdens or targets? How could you move toward viewing people as God's beloved children who matter and need your help?

4. Is your church truly Jesus centered? Where do you see more of a reliance on church-growth techniques or on sermons based on practical advice instead of trusting and preaching Jesus?

5. In what way does your church give people keys? How do you help people (especially those who might be newer) know that they are needed?
6. In what way does your church give tees? How do you help people (especially those who might be newer) know that they are known and loved?

CHAPTER 12

Creating Systems That Empower *It*

*You don't rise to the level of your goals, you fall to the
level of your systems.*

—James Clear

G oals.

You now have some goals. Right? I know after I read a
book like this, I have a list of goals I'm ready to go after. With this
book's end in sight, you might have some goals like:

1. Create more camaraderie on our staff.
2. Teach our leaders that failure is acceptable and a path to
   learning.
3. Get our people more outward focused.

Goals are good. I'm a fan of goals. But goals are not the solution.
Goals do not determine success.

You already know this, though you may not have thought of it
that way.

How do you know it? Because you realize that most people, and
most churches, have pretty similar goals but vastly different results.
Isn't it true?

People have about the same health goals. I bet you don't know anyone who has goals of achieving super-high cholesterol and dying in their fifties of a heart attack.

People have similar financial goals. You have no friends with the goals of being constantly stressed about money and going bankrupt by age forty-five.

People have nearly identical marriage goals. You don't know anyone who has goals of arguing all the time and divorcing after the kids are out of middle school but sometime before they go to college.

No. Our goals are basically the same. Everyone wants to lose the extra weight, experience financial freedom, and be happily married.

The same is true with churches. No church has these goals:

1. Fight over worship style and carpet color.
2. Encourage decreasing offerings.
3. Have more people dying than being born, and more people leaving the church than getting baptized.

No. Every church wants to preach the gospel to all creation, make disciples of all nations, experience Acts 2 community, and have taste-of-heaven worship.

So why is it that we have pretty similar goals but vastly different results? It's obviously not the goals. Goals do not determine success.

What does?

Systems.

Now that we have our seven leadership ingredients that lead to *it,* how do we apply them to do ministry in an effective way? We create systems that empower and sustain *it.*

Systems.

Churches that have *it* create the systems that sustain it.

If you are not achieving your goals, the issue is not your goals, it's your systems.

> **Churches that have *it* create the systems that sustain it.**

If you are having problems in your ministry, the problem is likely related to your systems.

If you always find yourself complaining that there are not enough hours in the day or are always putting out fires or have a confused staff that doesn't know who is responsible for what, the problem is your systems.

We tend to blame our people. If we just had better people, we would have better results. If we had *it* people, we would have *it*.

The issue is not your people. The problem is your systems.

A Tale of Two Chicken Restaurants

Charles Dickens' famous novel *A Tale of Two Cities* starts, "It was the best of times, it was the worst of times, it was the age of wisdom, it was the age of foolishness, it was the epoch of belief, it was the epoch of incredulity, it was the season of light, it was the season of darkness, it was the spring of hope, it was the winter of despair."

I don't even know what an epoch is, but I would like to tell you a tale of two chicken restaurants. The story starts like this: "It was the best of chicken restaurants, it became the worst of chicken restaurants, it was the age of wings, it was the age of fryers, it was the epoch of belief in a new restaurant and the epoch of incredulity at an old one, it was the season of light (meat), it was the season of dark (meat), it was the spring of hope, it was the restroom of despair."

I want to illustrate the power of systems by comparing two chicken restaurants.

One I have to talk bad about, so I'll change the name. When I was growing up, Grandma's Chicken (not the real name) was the place to go. Everyone wanted to eat their chicken-fried steak and mashed potatoes with gravy and green beans. They had a grandma (not her real name) who would go around in a cute little grandma apron giving out biscuits with honey and butter. The food was "slap your grandma good." (If you have never heard this phrase before, Urban Dictionary says it means that "something is so good that you're awestruck by it to the point where you're so disoriented that you might mistakenly slap your grandmother.")

I had not seen a Grandma's Chicken restaurant for probably twenty years when one day I had all six kids in the car and we drove past one. I lit up. "Guys! You are not going to believe this place! You are going to love it!" I corralled all six kids and rushed them into the restaurant, anticipating their being awestruck to the point of disorientation by how much they would love Grandma's Chicken.

The first thing I noticed was that no one was behind the counter. We waited until finally a teenager came out and acted annoyed that we were there. I wondered if maybe we were interrupting her makeout time with her boyfriend in the kitchen. She took our order, though it was difficult for her to get it right and she was rude the whole time. After ordering, we sat down and waited for God to send apron-clad Grandma with the biscuits from heaven. Grandma never came. There was no grandma, no biscuits, no honey, no butter. Finally, our order arrived. It was not so good. My kids looked at me like I was delusional or had early onset dementia. I got up, brokenhearted, went to the bathroom, and my feet stuck to the floor. Nasty! I always think dirty bathroom equals dirty kitchen, but I had to banish that thought from my mind because I was already feeling a little sick.

A couple of years later, we drove past another Grandma's Chicken in a different town. I announced that the one we had been to must be the exception. This one would be better. This one would take me and my family back to the glory days as I remembered them. It did not. It was an almost identically bad experience as the last time.

Contrast that with the second chicken restaurant: Chick-fil-A. Years ago when we were in Florida, we took all six kids into this restaurant we had never been to with the kind of funny name. Our kids were little and running around everywhere, scurrying into the fast-food restaurant looking like six drunk squirrels. A lady came out from behind the counter and, in an appropriate, loving way, asked if she could help with our kids. I told her, "You can have my kids!" She took our baby, Joy, and put her in a little baby seat. She gave a balloon and a toy to my toddlers. We're ordering, and this employee is babysitting my kids! Everything about the experience was amazing. The building was spotless. The atmosphere felt fun and alive. The employees were delightful and friendly and seemed to love their jobs and sincerely care about us. The food came out quickly and was addictively delicious. The staff refilled our drinks like we were dining in a full-service restaurant. It wasn't just good service, it was truly exceptional.

I discovered that the franchise owner was sitting at a booth in the corner, so I went over and told him he should double the pay of his amazing employees. He recognized me from a leadership conference I had spoken at, thanked me for investing in leaders, and gave me ten coupons for free chicken sandwiches!

I was so blown away by the whole experience that I wrote about it in the blog I had at that time. Somehow the CEO of Chick-fil-A heard about it and sent me an autographed copy of his book with twenty coupons for free chicken sandwiches!

Question: Why was my experience at Grandma's so terrible and at Chick-fil-A so incredible? Most people would answer, "The people."

No. I would bet you that the inept employees at Grandma's could have been excellent employees at Chick-fil-A, and the successful employees at Chick-fil-A might have struggled at Grandma's.

Why?

Because the issue is not people. The problem is systems.

Strong systems make good people look great. Weak systems make great people look bad.

How You Accomplish What

What is a system? A system is how you accomplish the *what*.

The *what* is the goal. It's what you hope to achieve. Again, every pastor's and church leader's *what* is basically the same. What differentiates those who get *it* and those who don't is the *how*.

We could say it this way: Systems create behaviors. Behaviors become habits. Habits drive outcomes. So if you want better outcomes, create better systems. Good news: small changes in your systems can create big changes in your outcomes.

You know those churches with the big numbers? So much of it is driven by their systems. They are crystal clear about what they want to accomplish. And they have prayerfully created the best plan to consistently bring about the desired spiritual results. Churches that have *it* create the systems that sustain it. It's the small things no one sees that bring the results everyone wants.

Systems create behaviors. Behaviors become habits. Habits drive outcomes.

I just looked Chick-fil-A up online. In the 2010s, they increased their revenue 15 percent per year, while the rest of the industry grew by only 3.4 percent. They have opened more stores than other chains. And even while opening more stores, in 2018, Chick-fil-A had an average of $4.7 million in sales per store, well above the $1.3 to $2.8 million average for most of their peers.[9]

Those are goals everyone has, results everyone wants. How does Chick-fil-A get them? It's the small things no one sees. It's the way they train employees that produces their customer service that wows first-time guests like me, that leads those customers to come back time and time again.

It's all about their systems.

Intent or Default

You might be thinking, *I'm still not positive what you mean. I don't think we really have any systems.*

I would tell you, respectfully, that you do.

Your system might be: Drive to the church building. Unlock the doors and turn on the lights. Respond to problems all day. Turn off the lights and lock the doors. Drive away from the church building.

That's a system. It's not one that will create the results you are hoping for, but it *is* a system.

The truth is, you have systems either by intent or by default, but you have them.

Your system came about because you strategically created it or because of apathy and by accident. It's time to stop tolerating and start creating, to design a system that leaves little to chance, to create a detailed plan of who does what, when, and how.

I mentioned how all of our campuses are very similar. The reason is because we have a system.

As I write this, our church meets in more than forty locations and is 100 percent debt free. When we launch a campus, we already have the money to pay for the building without borrowing. In one calendar year, we started five new locations in five states. We funded five 36,000-square-foot buildings that seat about eight hundred people each.

There was a day when it was painfully difficult for our church to add a service. We would freak out about whether we had enough volunteers and whether we could get it done. Launching services used to feel overwhelming, but now we can successfully launch new locations.

What happened? Systems happened.

We created really good systems. We have a launch process we use before we start a campus.

In the following graphic, you'll see items like initial meetings, which are the same for every new Life.Church campus. At each location, we buy the exact same products from the same vendors. We've tested them over time and know they work. The landscaping team and the janitorial service crew and the stage design and tech teams come in to establish their systems at the same time for every campus. The count team is trained in the same way at the same time.

That system was created with intention, and it was not developed overnight. When we started, our campus launch approach was much more haphazard. Remember what happened? We had to close church campuses in Phoenix because they just couldn't make it.

If you want a better outcome, you need a better system. Create a system designed to get the results you want.

What's Your What?

Maybe I've convinced you and you're wondering, *Where do we start?*

You start with your *what*. To get your what, you need the right *how*, but to establish the right how, you need to know your what. (I think I just graduated from Dr. Seuss University!)

I said it's not about the goal, it's about the system. That's true. But you want to design your system to achieve a specific goal. So your *what* must be clearly defined and communicated. We've already talked about the power of vision, so we'll move on. But *you* can't move on till you know what your what is.

Let me share another example. A while back, at Life.Church we decided we needed to have more of an evangelistic and inviting culture. The what: we wanted our people to be inspired to invite their friends to Life.Church. That was the goal, but it's not about the goal, it's about the system. The system is the how. So how would we inspire our people?

Launch Team

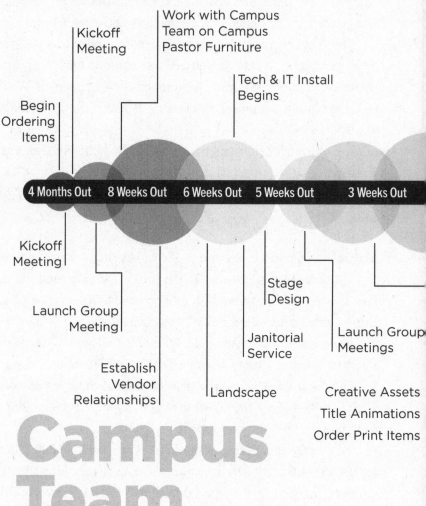

Begin
Ordering
Items

Kickoff
Meeting

Work with Campus
Team on Campus
Pastor Furniture

Tech & IT Install
Begins

| 4 Months Out | 8 Weeks Out | 6 Weeks Out | 5 Weeks Out | 3 Weeks Out |

Kickoff
Meeting

Launch Group
Meeting

Establish
Vendor
Relationships

Stage
Design

Janitorial
Service

Landscape

Launch Group
Meetings

Creative Assets

Title Animations

Order Print Items

Campus Team

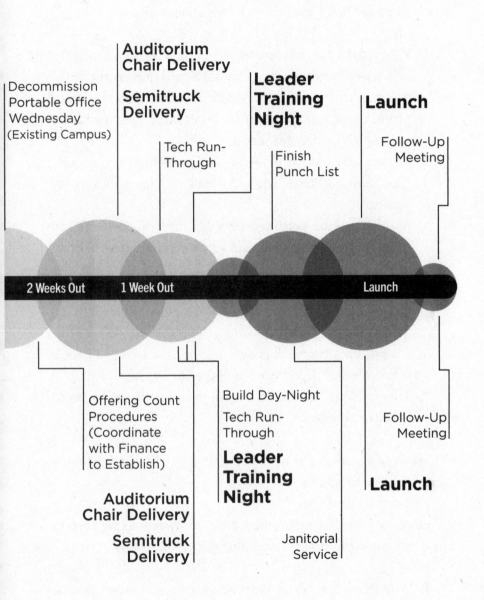

Decommission
Portable Office
Wednesday
(Existing Campus)

**Auditorium
Chair Delivery**

**Semitruck
Delivery**

Tech Run-
Through

**Leader
Training
Night**

Finish
Punch List

Launch

Follow-Up
Meeting

2 Weeks Out   1 Week Out   Launch

Offering Count
Procedures
(Coordinate
with Finance
to Establish)

**Auditorium
Chair Delivery**

**Semitruck
Delivery**

Build Day-Night

Tech Run-
Through

**Leader
Training
Night**

Janitorial
Service

Follow-Up
Meeting

Launch

We set up a seven-touch system designed to encourage our people to invite their friends to each new sermon series:

1. We mailed a card to everyone in our database explaining the new series. Note: We didn't send the card to everyone in the community. That wouldn't be bad, but our goal was to get our people excited about the series and to invite their friends, so we sent the card to our people.
2. The weekend prior, we showed a video promoting the new series.
3. That same weekend, I talked about the new series in my message.
4. At the end of the worship experience, the local pastors talked about the upcoming series and why it was important to bring others to hear it.
5. We placed an invitation card on every seat, knowing our people could use it as an evangelism tool by placing it in the hands of an unchurched friend.
6. We put up a banner highlighting the new series so people would see it as they drove out of the parking lot.
7. All week long, we used all of our social media platforms to hype the new series.

See how it works? You need to know your what, and then you create a system to achieve it.

Let's dig a little deeper.

Once we know our what, there are three questions we need to answer to create the systems for the people on our teams.

1. *What should be expected?* What do we expect from our greeters, our follow-up team, the people in our kids' ministry, our student ministry volunteers, and our tech crew? What do we want to see in our culture? What mindsets, focuses, and attitudes?

Remember, we're designing a system that leaves little to chance. We want a detailed plan of who does what, when, and how.

2. *What should be rewarded?* We are clear on exactly what behavior is a win. We celebrate when we see the qualities or behaviors we expect. *That's exactly it! Way to go! Thank you! I'm proud of you!* People love to be celebrated and will do what you reward.

3. *What should be corrected?* When someone steps out of the system or out of our values or out of our culture, we can't ignore that. We need to talk about it and correct it.

So we have an expectation and we both reward and correct behavior. The problem is that too often what is rewarded and corrected is not consistent with what's expected.

A clear example of this is bad parenting. Not that I have ever been guilty of bad parenting. Okay, I fall into bad-parenting mode just like everyone else. When I do, I start announcing new goals "Everyone will turn their phones off by 10:00 p.m.!"—and two nights later, some of the kids don't do it and I'm like, "You'll do what I say. I'm going to count to three and that phone better be off! . . . Okay, I'm going to count to thirty! . . . Fine, we can go get ice cream if you turn your phone off . . . Do you like your ice cream? Wait, did you turn your phone off?!" Inside, I'm thinking, *Groeschel, you know better. You can't negotiate with terrorists!*

What's the problem? Perhaps a not-well-thought-out what, and definitely not holding people accountable for what's expected. We need to create a system that rewards people when they do what we expect and corrects them when they don't.

For instance, let's say you decide that you want every new person who shows up at your church to receive a welcome text within twelve hours. If you make it clear who needs to do what to make that happen, and you reward the people who do it and correct those who don't, a system will emerge.

Healthy systems facilitate *it*. Healthy systems never happen by accident. They happen with intentionality. It takes hard work to create the processes that make the right *how* clear, but once they're established, your life will be easier. You will have automated what you want to happen. Behavior that was once challenging to get people to do will become difficult to get people not to do. That's why whenever you see a church that has *it*, you'll see the systems that help create and sustain it.

You might argue, "But what about the Holy Spirit, the anointing, the power of God? Systems aren't spiritual." While we always undeniably need the Holy Spirit and the anointing and power of God, systems are profoundly spiritual. When God spoke and created the world, he created . . . wait for it . . . a solar system. For some pastors, the most spiritual thing you could do is to get organized.

Quality, consistency, and success are never accidents. They happen because of healthy systems. But it takes time, effort, and intentionality. Healthy systems never happen by accident. No pastor has ever said, "Whoops, I ate breakfast, walked my dog, and what?! Presto! We had clear, healthy, God-honoring systems." You might be realizing, "We don't have a follow-up problem, we have a systems problem." Or, "We don't have an excellence problem, we have a systems problem." You know correcting the problem will take a lot of work and energy. You might not feel like you have the time. Remember, if you are too busy to create the right systems, you will *always* be too busy. You do have the time, and it's time to get disciplined!

To Floss or Not to Floss, That Is the Discipline

Flossing changed my life.

I hate flossing. (Doesn't everyone?) But to the delight of dental hygienists everywhere, flossing changed my life.

Why? Because flossing did not come naturally to me, so I had to create a system to automate flossing. Every time I floss, it tells me that I am disciplined.

Similarly, I have a system in which I wake up early every morning and do my YouVersion Bible study. I take in God's Word, which helps conform me to the image of Christ.

Then I get in to work early and I'm productive. Other people start arriving, and it makes me feel good to know I have already accomplished a lot because of the system I have disciplined myself to live by.

I bring the same healthy foods to work every day, and I leave work a little early and am at the gym at 4:00, usually six or seven days a week. I'm healthy, and the reason is a system I created.

I get home from work and get to spend the night with my wife. She's happy, and it led to our having *six* kids, and it's all because I floss.

If I didn't floss, I wouldn't feel so disciplined, which might lead me to stay up too late. If I stayed up too late, I might not get up early to do my Bible study. I would probably get to church late. I'd be annoyed all day, wouldn't be very productive, would have to work later, wouldn't get to the gym, would leave work realizing that Amy was going to be mad because I worked late, and so I'd speed home and get pulled over by a police officer. I wouldn't want the ticket, so I'd try to outrun the police and get arrested and put in jail. Why? Because I didn't floss.

Okay, that may be a slight exaggeration. But never underestimate what God can do through one small habit. Never underestimate what God can do when instead of just having a goal, you are disciplined about creating and living by a system that is the how for your what. I love the encouragement we get in Zechariah 4:10: "Do not despise these small beginnings, for the LORD rejoices to see the work begin" (NLT).

Never underestimate what God can do through one small habit.

Goals. Goals are good. I'm a fan of goals. But goals are not the solution. Goals do not determine success. Systems do. So start creating the right systems—the how that will get you to your what. It might not feel significant, but do not despise small beginnings and never underestimate what God can do with one small habit. Define the what, then decide what should be expected, what should be rewarded, and what should be corrected. Start living by those systems and watch *it* happen.

My Pen Collection

I said that after reading a book like this it's typical to have a list of goals. "We're going to reach more people. Our church is going to grow. We're gonna see more baptisms. Our small group attendance will increase next year."

I've had similar goals over the years and still have some today. But since we're talking about goals, I want to encourage you to consider a different type of goal. Most people make "do" goals: this is what I want to do. But I'd encourage you to start with "who" goals. Instead of just focusing on what you hope to do and accomplish, let's start with who you want to be. At the top of that who list, I'm hoping you have a goal to be faithful. Nothing is more *it* than faithfulness.

In 2005, I received a pen. The pen had my name on it and the year: 2005. I have never been a collector of pens, so I was a little confused by this gift. Then I read the note. It was written by another pastor, kind of a hero of mine. The note was written with the pen I was receiving. This pastor explained that the pen represented another year of serving Jesus, being faithful to my wife, and serving my church with integrity.

I received another pen the next year, and another the year after that. After about six years, it became very meaningful. I looked forward to receiving that pen.

After about ten years, I met the pastor who sent them. As we talked, I asked him about the pens. How many pens did he send out? He said that he used to send a lot, but many of the pastors he used to send them to no longer served in ministry.

It broke my heart. I could imagine these pastors who had burned out or made decisions that led them to marital unfaithfulness or a lack of financial integrity. I even thought of friends of mine who might be some of the pastors who could no longer receive the pens.

I knew that I would not trade all of the church-growth success in the world for the honor of getting one of those pens each year, because more than anything, I want to be faithful.

I also realized that I am a weak, fallen human being who is vulnerable to the same temptations and bad decisions as those pastors who made decisions I'm sure they regret. We all started with the same goals. I don't know any pastor whose goals are to slowly lose their focus on God and drift away from their first love for Jesus, and to make decisions that will embarrass their Lord, their family, and their church.

No. Every pastor wants to stay close to God and live by the power of the Spirit and honor their family and someday hear, "Well done, good and faithful servant."

So why is it that church leaders have pretty similar goals but vastly different results? It's obviously not the goals. Goals do not lead to faithfulness.

What does?

Systems.

Hearing my pen benefactor tell me that many pastors weren't receiving pens anymore made me thankful for, and more committed to, the systems I have put in my life. The disciplines of reading my Bible every day, creating space to pray passionate prayers, having accountability in my life, being part of Christ's body, giving the first 10 percent of everything I take in back to God and then giving generously from there.

That's why I work hard to remind myself that I am not successful when I achieve some desired goal a few weeks, months, or years from now. I am successful when I've been faithful and obedient to God *today*. Don't get down on yourself if your church doesn't have *it* at this moment. Just do what you know might lead to it. Prayerfully define what you would like to see in your church. Define who does what, and when and how. Celebrate when you see *it*. Correct when you don't. Be faithful even when no one else is watching. Remember, it's the things no one sees that bring the results everyone wants. You won't be successful someday when you see the results. You are successful when you are obedient and faithful *today*.

One of the Bible heroes of faithfulness is Daniel. This dude was able to stand down hungry lions and to live a holy life in a culture that demanded he leave it behind. How? We get an insight in Daniel 6. Daniel learns that the king has decreed that anyone who prays to God will be executed. What does he do in response? "But when Daniel learned that the law had been signed, he went home and knelt down as usual in his upstairs room, with its windows open toward Jerusalem. He prayed three times a day, just as he had always done, giving thanks to his God" (v. 10 NLT).

Did you notice?

You probably noticed Daniel's courage in praying when he knew it could lead to his death.

But did you notice? Daniel prayed "just as he had always done."

He wasn't faithful because he had set a goal of being faithful. Everyone sets a goal of being faithful. Daniel was faithful because he had created a system that led to faithfulness. His system was praying three times a day, toward Jerusalem, window open, giving thanks to God. Years of disciplining himself to live by that system strengthened his relationship with God and built his intimacy with and trust in him. The result? He was faithful. He got the pen.

Goals don't determine success.

Systems do.

It Factors

- Goals do not determine success. Systems do.
- We don't have people problems. We have system problems.
- Strong systems make good people look great. Weak systems make great people look bad.
- We need to stop tolerating and start creating.
- Systems create behaviors. Behaviors become habits. Habits drive outcomes.
- A system is a set of principles or procedures that determines how something is done.
- Healthy systems never happen by accident.
- Too often what is rewarded or corrected is not consistent with what's expected.
- Never underestimate how God can start something big through one small habit.
- The ultimate *it* is faithfulness.

Questions for Discussion or Reflection

1. What systems exist in your ministry?
2. Were those systems created intentionally or by default?
3. It has been said that your systems are perfectly designed to get the results they're getting. Are you happy with the results your systems are getting?
4. What new system do you need to create to move you toward your goals?
5. For that system, who needs to do what?
6. How will you reward and correct to reinforce the behavior you're expecting?

CHAPTER 13

Centered around *It*

*Stay centered in your leadership through intention,
appreciation, and communication.*
—**Bobbie Goheen**

When I was eight years old, my parents took me to the Barnum and Bailey Circus. I was impressed by the elephants, amazed by the lion tamer, and a little freaked out by the clowns, but the moment when I totally lost it was when the tightrope walker came out. This half-crazed legend fearlessly inched his way across a wire that seemed to be a half mile off the ground. The crowd was wowed, I dropped my popcorn, and the course of my life was altered. His ability to balance, to stay centered, was beyond inspirational. I knew I no longer wanted to be just a professional baseball player and an astronaut. I wanted to be a professional baseball player and an astronaut and a tightrope walker!

I practiced walking across fence ledges and tree limbs and the top of swing sets. Unfortunately, it seemed like my dream was not meant to be.

Until years later on a family trip to Colorado. Several young, adventurous, and ridiculously cool twentysomethings had strung a line of flexible webbing between two trees. But instead of tightrope walking, these guys were slacklining. One guy bounced his way to the middle, jumped like he was on a trampoline, did a flip, and landed perfectly back on the line.

My kids were in awe, and I realized this was my chance. Like a montage scene from *Karate Kid,* I remembered my years (okay, it was a couple of days) of training to be a tightrope walker. It hit me: *Who knows but that I have come to Colorado for such a time as this?* I asked the cool bros if I could try it. They looked at me, trying not to laugh, and agreed. I got in position and paused, telling myself, *All you have to do is balance. Just stay centered, Groeschel.* Suddenly, I could hear music. It may have only been in my head, but it was *my* song: "You're the best! Around! Nothing's gonna ever keep you down!" I took one confident step and the line swung out from under me and shot me like a cannon straight down into the ground.

When it came to tightrope walking and slacklining, turns out I wanted it, but I did not have it.

What do you do when you know you don't have *it,* but you want it?

You may see other church leaders who have *it,* that something special that is hard to define but impossible to miss. You long to have the impact they have, build a church like they lead, reach people others aren't reaching. But it just seems out of reach to you. Perhaps you find it hard to relate to their giftedness or their situation.

Good news: *it* is always a work of God. Yes, God does it through people. But *it* cannot be packaged, produced with human effort, or purchased. God does it, through people, and God can choose anyone he wants to use for his glory. God can choose *you.* I believe he wants to.

Although we can never lure, bribe, or trick God into doing more through us, we *can* position ourselves to be stronger candidates for God to choose. *You* can position yourself. But it's not easy. And, it turns out, it has everything to do with keeping your balance and staying centered. Staying centered is how we put ourselves in the place where God is more likely to give *it,* and how we live out our seven leadership ingredients as we get it.

We need to be centered around *it.* If you are prepared to do some hard work, I'll explain. But remember, I warned you.

In Spirit

Leaders who have *it* don't just motivate, they inspire.

Don't get me wrong, there is nothing wrong with motivating. But motivating implies getting people to do something they would rather not do. You might motivate someone to eat right, exercise, or stay late at work to finish the job. Motivating implies pushing.

Inspiring (which comes from the root "in-spirit") means to pull out the best. Instead of pushing people to do what they don't really want to do, leaders who have *it* tend to inspire people so they want and choose to do what is right. You pull out their team-player, missional, kingdom-focused hearts. When you inspire others, you will likely get more from them than you expected. Research shows that employees who describe themselves as inspired are more than twice as productive as those who call themselves satisfied.[10]

When I talk about inspiring, chances are you might envision giving an inspirational speech. You might picture your favorite coach rousing the team with an emotionally charged halftime talk. Or you might think back on that one graduation address that held every student and parent captive. Or it could be that viral TED Talk that moved you to change something significant in your life.

Your next thought might be, *But I could never inspire like that. If I have to be inspirational to have it, I guess I never will.*

Let me be clear. Charismatic, charge-the-hill, conquer-the-enemy, take-no-prisoners speeches are a tool some leaders use to inspire. But it is just one of many tools available in a leader's toolbox, and it's not the most important one. Leaders who have *it* understand this.

Bain & Company surveyed more than two thousand employees and made a staggering discovery that can help you get *it* and keep it in your leadership. They discovered there are thirty-three attributes leaders can use to inspire their teams. (See pages 198–99.)

Without covering the whole list, let's highlight a few qualities that might come naturally to you:

- If you have an optimistic outlook, you can easily inspire your staff or volunteers to do more to make a difference in the world.
- If you exhibit a consistent and genuine posture of humility, you are a prime candidate to help others believe in God's call on their lives.
- If you are gifted to see the big picture, you can look at a situation and see clearly what needs to be done, and people are more likely to follow you.
- If you set a tone of confidence and trust, you can move people to targeted action.
- If you are generous in giving recognition or lead with genuine empathy, you can consistently bring out the best in people.

These are all great qualities, but one stands head and shoulders above the rest. Research shows that the most inspirational leaders, those who have *it*, are centered in their leadership. They are secure, grounded, confident. Centered leaders are fully engaged, internally aligned, and outwardly clear. They are guided by values, driven by a purpose, and obsessed with their mission.

It's not common for us to talk this way or to use the word *centered*. Most staff members never say, "My last boss wasn't centered.

But my new one really is!" Few church members will ever tell you, "Now that we have a centered pastor, God is starting to move."

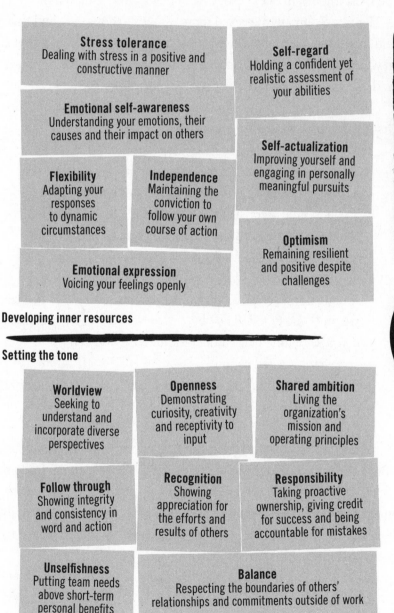

Stress tolerance
Dealing with stress in a positive and constructive manner

Self-regard
Holding a confident yet realistic assessment of your abilities

Emotional self-awareness
Understanding your emotions, their causes and their impact on others

Self-actualization
Improving yourself and engaging in personally meaningful pursuits

Flexibility
Adapting your responses to dynamic circumstances

Independence
Maintaining the conviction to follow your own course of action

Optimism
Remaining resilient and positive despite challenges

Emotional expression
Voicing your feelings openly

Developing inner resources

Setting the tone

Centeredn

Worldview
Seeking to understand and incorporate diverse perspectives

Openness
Demonstrating curiosity, creativity and receptivity to input

Shared ambition
Living the organization's mission and operating principles

Follow through
Showing integrity and consistency in word and action

Recognition
Showing appreciation for the efforts and results of others

Responsibility
Taking proactive ownership, giving credit for success and being accountable for mistakes

Unselfishness
Putting team needs above short-term personal benefits

Balance
Respecting the boundaries of others' relationships and commitments outside of work

They may not say it, but they often feel it. The absence of centered leadership demotivates. The presence of it inspires.

Vitality
Showing passion for your work and giving energy to others

Humility
Maintaining a balanced ego

Empathy
Understanding and appreciating others' needs and feelings

Development
Assisting others in advancing their skills

Assertiveness
Advocating your point of view in an open, honest and direct way

Listening
Paying true attention to others' comments, ideas and feelings

Expressiveness
Conveying ideas and emotions clearly and compellingly

Commonality
Sharing mutual interests and activities

Connecting with others

gaging
parts of
e mind to
come fully
esent

Leading the team

Vision
Creating a compelling objective that build confidence and encourages sign-up

Focus
Orienting teams toward the most relevant set of outcomes

Harmony
Fostering alignment and resolving conflicts

Direction
Setting the appropriate group and individual expectations

Servanthood
Investing on behalf of others and finding joy in their success

Empowerment
Allowing and encouraging the freedom to stretch

Co-creation
Trusting that collaboration can yield better results

Sponsorship
Engaging to help others achieve their broad career aspirations

Used with permission from Bain & Company (www.bain.com).

Uncentered

If you have been around long, you've witnessed some uncentered leaders. They come in all different shapes and sizes. You might meet one who is a control freak. Others are disengaged, passive, and uninvolved. Some are domineering. There are uncentered leaders who are nonconfrontational people pleasers. Some are risk-takers with no sense of reality. Others are afraid to make a move. No two uncentered leaders look alike. But the feeling you get from them never changes.

Uncentered leaders create unsettled followers.

If you have ever served under an uncentered leader, a leader without *it*, you likely wanted to buy into the vision, tried to buy into the vision, but you just couldn't.

On the other hand, leaders who have *it* are centered. What they have is difficult to describe, but impossible to miss. Your coworkers will never say, "Our pastor was off center for a while. He seemed to lean slightly to the left. Finally, he's on track and centered again."

They won't say it, but they will feel it. A team knows whether or not the leader is centered. The centered leader who has *it* leads with a quiet and assured calm. He or she has an inward compass. Their confidence is contagious. The team is inspired by the leader's resolve.

The centered leader who has *it* leads with a quiet and assured calm.

Are you a centered leader?

Bad news: if you are not centered, you are not fooling anyone.

Good news: if you are not centered, if you don't have *it*, you can become centered and you can get it.

The Three Offenses of Off-Center Leadership

If you have worked with an off-center leader, you've observed one or more of the significant downsides. Let's talk about the three offenses of off-center leadership and examine each closely. A warning: You will likely see at least one in your own leadership. It's hard to admit, but more dangerous to ignore.

1. *Off-center leaders are annoyingly insecure.* Have you been around an insecure leader? They rarely say it out loud, but their actions scream, "Tell me I'm good. Tell me you like me. I'm a good leader, right?" The insecure leader often comes across as needy. She might avoid conflict. He might seem to consistently lack the resolve to make hard decisions or stick with a plan.

   Some insecure leaders may not look it, but they are actually the most unsettled. Sometimes their insecurity manifests itself as arrogance. Instead of being passive, these insecure leaders often bully others, micromanage, or are all-around know-it-all jerks. These leaders who lack *it* and don't get it tend to take all the credit and give all the blame. They are hard to work for and even harder to believe in. Their negative impact is real, and the cost is high.

   When the leader lacks confidence, the team lacks commitment. Eventually the team grows weaker. Why? Insecure leaders tend to produce insecure followers.

2. *Off-center leaders are consistently unpredictable.* If you follow a leader who doesn't have *it,* you never know what to expect. They are often unsettled and unsure. The only thing the team knows for certain is that the direction will change. Soon there will be a new project, new initiative, new program, new strategy, new focus, new emphasis, or new solution.

   An unpredictable leader may try to empower you by delegating authority to you and giving you freedom to lead, only to take it back and leave you confused. Your leader may encourage you, then criticize you, then repeat the process until you always feel on edge. Again, the cost of this offense is high. Unpredictable leaders produce hesitant followers. You feel like you have to walk around on eggshells. You're forced to play it safe. If you have an idea, you probably keep it to yourself. Experience has taught you not to rock the boat.

3. *Off-center leaders are distastefully self-absorbed.* Leaders who lack *it* have a way of sucking the life out of the best people. The self-absorbed leader is all about self. It's *their* team. It's *their* vision. What you do is a means to their end, their goals, their well-being.

   You have likely witnessed a domineering, narcissistic leader who cannot talk about much besides themselves. You feel like a supporting actor in someone else's story. Over time, everyone loses under this type of leadership. Self-absorbed leaders produce resentful followers. You know when a leader doesn't truly care about you. Even though they don't, you want to care, but discover you can't, at least not for long. I had a friend who worked for a self-absorbed leader. He wanted to give his best, but he got increasingly discouraged and resentful. I remember him saying of his boss, "He can buy my time, but he can't buy my heart."

Leaders who lack *it,* who are off-center, produce insecure, hesitant, and resentful followers. You may have noticed more than one problem in the previous sentence. It's not just the adjectives that are a problem (insecure, hesitant, resentful). It's also the noun they modify (followers). That's another quality that sets apart truly centered leaders. Centered leaders do not create followers. They create leaders. You reproduce what you are. Leaders who have *it* create other leaders who have it and, in so doing, continually multiply it.

So how do you get *it* in your leadership? I'm so glad you asked.

Getting Centered

Here is where the rubber meets the road. I'm going to ask you to be prayerfully open and honest and then to do something with what God shows you.

My guess is you are a little off center. So am I. We all are. This is as much of a theological issue as it is a practical one. Scripture makes it clear that we are all sinners. The Greek word for sin, *harmartia,* is an archery term that means to miss the target. When we sin, we are off center. Our sin nature impacts every area of our lives, including our leadership.

Remember the three offenses of off-center leadership. Leaders who are off center are:

1. annoyingly insecure
2. consistently unpredictable
3. distastefully self-absorbed

Most leaders (and I am no exception) have at least small doses of at least two of these challenges. It's likely that one stands out as your greatest growth opportunity. I'm going to ask you to choose just one area to develop. Asking God to help you in this area could transform you into a more centered spiritual leader. If you are working through this book with others, you can ask them to pray for you and hold you accountable. This one change could prepare you to get all of *it* that God wants to give you. God can multiply your growth in this area, so it has a cascading impact in other areas of your leadership.

So let's do it! Which one is your area for growth? Pray about it if necessary, but I'm guessing you already know. If you are writing in your book, why don't you circle it in the list? If you are listening to the audio book, why don't you say it out loud? Someone may look at you funny. That's okay. Just smile back. You might tell them, "It happens, and it *is* happening."

Got it named? Good.

Now let's walk through what it might look like to grow in each of the three areas.

Inwardly Confident

Leaders who have *it* are different. Instead of being annoyingly insecure, the centered leader is inwardly confident. That might seem like bad news to you because you think of yourself as unworthy, incapable, or unprepared. You could feel like you are too young, too green, too inexperienced. Or you might worry you are too old. I felt too young for years. Now I'm on the other end. When was I just right? I must have missed it!

Instead of being annoyingly insecure, the centered leader is inwardly confident.

If it's not your age, your spiritual enemy will give you other reasons to doubt yourself. You don't have the education. You are the "wrong" gender for your role. You are not married. You are not an extrovert. You are not intellectual enough. You are not a great speaker. You don't have the experience. You don't have the look (whatever that means). There is no end to the list of excuses your enemy can dish out and tempt you to believe.

The good news is that there is no excuse God can't overcome. There is no habit he can't change. There is no stronghold he cannot break. You don't have to be confident in yourself, your gifts, your talents, or your resume. You can find your confidence in him.

Confidence in yourself can be shallow and fleeting. You'd be surprised by how many leaders appear confident, but it's a facade. Confidence in yourself can be cheerleader confidence. You know what I mean? Have you ever watched a basketball game, and your team is losing by thirty points with only minutes left, but your cheerleaders are still chanting, "V-I-C-T-O-R-Y!" It's like, "Do you keep up on current events? Do you ever check on what's going on in the game?" Confidence in yourself can be unconvincing and even a denial of reality.

But confidence in God is substantial and enduring. Confidence is not about having incredible fashion sense and a budget to match. It's not about being the most charismatic, most eloquent, or best looking. And it's not just for those who have "arrived." I think the truth is we never arrive. Confidence comes not from mastering leadership or preaching but from being open to the work of God. Remember how Paul came to the Corinthians in weakness and fear, without eloquent preaching, but with confidence? Why? He attributed his confidence to "the Spirit's power" and having faith not in anything human "but on God's power." (See 1 Corinthians 2:3–5.) Knowing that God is working in me gives me confidence. You can have that same confidence.

Neediness repels. Confidence attracts. Ask God to help you grow in a confidence that is founded in him.

In this journey, you might consider asking God to give you a skill to develop, a weakness to accept, or a belief to change.

If it's a skill to develop, let's name it. Maybe it is time to become a better listener, to learn to give feedback, or to better prioritize your time. Perhaps you should learn to read financial statements, run more effective meetings, or improve your ability to hold your team accountable. If you can define it, you can do it. What are you waiting for? Ask God to direct you to the right class, to lead you to the perfect book, to give you a good mentor. If you allow God to grow you in one area, your confidence will grow in all areas.

It might not be a skill to develop but instead a weakness to accept. One of the best ways to grow in confidence is to accept that you do not have to be amazing in every area. Accepting a weakness, choosing to be okay with not being great in a specific way, can be a confidence game changer.

With the best intentions, so many leaders spend enormous amounts of time and energy trying to develop a trait or skill God did not wire them to have. Rather than always focusing on what you cannot do, you can accept your weaknesses and be freed up to focus on what you *can* do. Instead of trying to do something they could never do well, centered leaders confidently delegate to other trusted leaders. Those other leaders feel valued, which grows their confidence.

You might consider this idea if you are a parent. If your child comes home with one A, a few Bs, and a D minus, like most parents, you might immediately home in on the D minus. You might spend more time working with your child on that subject or hire a tutor to bring up the D minus. While that may be a good strategy to raise your kid's grade, that won't help your child be successful in life. He or she isn't likely to change the world in the subject they barely pass. The same is true for you as a leader. Accepting your weaknesses frees you to pursue your strengths. John Zenger said, "Great leaders are not defined by the absence of weakness, but rather by the presence of clear strengths."

To grow in your inner confidence, you might have a skill to develop or a weakness to accept—or perhaps you have a belief to change. When your inner critic whispers that you aren't, you can't, and you won't, remind yourself that God says you are, you can, and, with his help, you will. Determine what limiting thought is holding you back and replace it with God's truth. If you are a follower of Jesus, you have the mind of Christ. You are eternally secure. You can do all things through him who gives you strength. Maybe you have a belief to change.

If you need help with this—and I think we all do—I have

written an entire book on it: *Winning the War in Your Mind: Change Your Thinking, Change Your Life.* I wrote that book because I have struggled with confidence almost my entire life. I've always felt insecure and unsure of myself as a leader, and even more as a preacher. I started preaching as a very young believer. I lacked confidence in my Bible knowledge. I was certain everyone could see I was not good enough. So before I preached, I started doing a personal ritual. I still do it to this day. As I stand on the platform, just before preaching, I take one big step forward. This step means more to me than I can describe. Why? In my mind, I'm stepping out of my insecurities, fears, doubts, and limitations. With that one bold step forward, I'm stepping into God's calling, anointing, and assignment for me to say what he wants to be said on that day.

One. Step. Forward.

Perhaps that's what you need to do. Take one step toward *it*. You might need to step into a skill to develop. Or you have found a weakness to accept. Or you are stepping out of your excuses into a new belief about yourself. You are stepping out of the shackles of the devil's lies and into God's divine calling for you. Can you feel it? Will you believe it?

God wants you to have *it*.

Take. One. Step. Forward.

Strategically Consistent

Many leaders are consistently unpredictable, but leaders who have *it* are strategically consistent. I love how CEO Jack Welch described this. He said, "Great leaders are both relentless and boring." That quote makes me feel good. Before I spoke at a leadership event recently, the host said about me, "Craig is one of the most boring leaders I've ever met." No kidding. He really said that! Then he explained, in one of the most meaningful introductions I've ever had, why my consistency was contagious in creating a compelling culture.

Many people assume that leaders who have *it* soar in, inspire wildly, and rocket off. Like Superman flying in to save the day, these superleaders have superpowers. They are faster than a changing economy. More powerful than a corporate takeover. Able to create tall profits in a single bound. The problem is Superman is not real, and neither are superleaders. The most successful generally aren't the ones who risk the most or swing the hardest. They are the leaders who show up and consistently do the right things over time.

Successful leaders do consistently what others do occasionally.

I've always told our team that successful leaders do consistently what others do occasionally.

To become more centered, perhaps you should simply be more consistent. I intentionally say the same things over and over again. The vision has not changed. The strategy is consistent. It might not go viral. It might not attract celebrities. But our team knows what to expect. They understand the plan. They embrace the strategy. They believe in the mission. And consistently lives are changed.

I like the way one of Google's former senior vice presidents described it. Think about the power behind these words. Laszlo Bock explained, "If a leader is consistent, people on their teams experience tremendous freedom, because then they know that within certain parameters, they can do whatever they want. If your manager is all over the place, you're never going to know what you can do, and you're going to experience it as very restrictive."[11] Find out what works and do it over and over again.

If this is your one area for growth, take a moment to think about where you might be sending mixed messages to your team. (If you are not sure, ask someone you trust.) Are you often tempted to compare? To look for greener pastures? To find the silver bullet? The new program? Sure, there are times when you want to be open to God leading you in a different direction, but God doesn't change his mind every six weeks. Perhaps you could grow in consistency. You might consistently run spiritually charged, engaging meetings. Or consistently celebrate and embrace those who create spiritual wins. Or consistently share the vision until your church is white hot with passion for the unsaved. Or wake up every day and consistently build leaders. You trust them. You empower them. You release them. You change the world through them.

Look around at the leaders who have *it*. In most cases, they are brilliantly and strategically consistent. Centered leaders are easy to follow. Consistent actions create consistent results. Consistent communication develops deep and lasting trust. Consistent values unite people with an unquenchable passion. It's not what you do occasionally that will make your ministry successful. It's what you do consistently.

Mission Driven

When I first heard Nick Harris preach, I was ready to quit my job in sales and do whatever he needed at First United Methodist Church. I would have volunteered, full time, but he talked me into keeping my job at Honeywell until the right door opened for ministry. Why was I willing to walk away from income to devote myself to a cause? Pastor Nick was the most mission-driven leader I had ever known.

Leaders who have *it* are consumed by a mission bigger than themselves. That burning drive, that unquenchable passion, often creates results. That's good, right? At first, yes. But success can create problems. One of the common pitfalls of success is when a leader starts to believe his or her own press. Oddly enough, a leader, church, or business does not even need to be wildly successful for a leader to

> Leaders who have *it* are consumed by a mission bigger than themselves.

become dangerously self-absorbed. Like gravity always pulls down, leadership success always sucks attention toward the leader. That attention and the power that can come with it can be intoxicating. If a leader doesn't push against that, then if they have *it,* they will lose it. If they don't have *it,* they will never get it.

To grow in your centeredness, to be a leader who has *it,* you want to be wholly consumed by your calling. What is your mission? It's way more than just what you do. The mission is why you do the what. Author and speaker Simon Sinek says, "People don't buy into what you do. They buy into why you do it." That's true. The why is what tends to attract *it.*

Take a moment to assess your personal missional buy-in. You might ask yourself, on a scale of one to ten, where would you rank your passion for the mission? What would your team say? If you would rank yourself lower than a ten, that is probably a strong indication of why you don't have *it* or are not likely to keep it.

Be warned, it is extremely challenging to be objective. It is hard to see complacency in a mirror. The most natural thing is to drift toward comfort. Rarely do we end up sacrificing for a cause bigger than ourselves by accident. Unless we fight hard against the natural flow toward comfort, we will likely sacrifice the mission for selfish pursuits.

If my words sound harsh or dramatic, it is only because I have personal experience with missional distractions. About fifteen years ago, when our church was experiencing a more difficult season, my team members gave me feedback in an anonymous 360 review. Several of them told me I was distracted and not leading as strongly as I had in the past. To me, they were not just wrong, they were dead wrong. I did care. I was engaged. Later, a different group gave me similar feedback. Stunned, I realized I had become blind to my own failures. The truth was I did care, but I had just written my first book, just spoken at my first big conference, and just started getting some attention from outside the church. Though I still loved the church, I did not realize how much the extra ministry had distracted me from my primary ministry. I had lost some missional passion.

What about you?

When Jesus called people to follow him, he did not say, "Come and give me a solid six. A seven is better, but I'll take what I can get." No, Jesus called people to carry a cross and give up their lives. He asked for nothing less than a ten. Those who said yes left *everything* to follow Jesus.

Jesus did not invite people to follow him on a mission of comfort. He never taught five steps to a happier life. He was bold and uncompromising in his mission. He came to seek and save the lost, to serve and not be served. He did not come for the healthy but for the sick. He did not come for the righteous but for the sinner. He came full of grace and truth. He came to set the captives free.

If you want your church to have *it,* the mission must stay front and center. It should burn within until the fire spreads to anyone close by. If you recognize that you have lost some of the passion, let's work to get it back. When Jesus was correcting the believers in Ephesus, he said, "Yet I hold this against you: You have forsaken the love you had at first" (Rev. 2:4). Jesus might say something similar to you. You did not lose it. You *left* it. Without meaning to, you left your first love. As someone once said, perhaps the way you are "doing the work of God is destroying the work of God in you." Jesus continued his loving rebuke and said, "Consider how far you have fallen! Repent and do the things you did at first" (v. 5).

Maybe it is time to go back to the basics. Remember why you started. Remember your salvation, the thrill of knowing your sins are forgiven. Remember the joy of seeing someone else meet Christ and be filled with the Holy Spirit, changed by grace, and overwhelmed with hope. Remember the first time God used you.

Remember when all you dreamed and prayed about was being used by God in the church. Now take a moment to grieve because you are complaining about the very thing you used to dream about. Repent and do the things you did at first.

The passion of the people won't exceed the passion of the leader. We don't want our people doing a job. We want them fulfilling a mission. Remember and embrace your why. People will work for a what, but they will give their lives for a why. If you want *it*, remember why you started. Fall in love with Christ's mission all over again.

Jesus Had *It*

Without a doubt, the most centered leader in the history of the world was Jesus. It is safe to say he was the only truly consistently centered leader. He never sinned. Never strayed. Never missed the target. Jesus always lived the will of his Father.

When you reflect on your leadership, which is the one area you want God to help you develop? Do you need to overcome your nagging insecurity and step into kingdom confidence? Do you need God's help to overcome your sinful pull toward inconsistency and allow his Spirit to empower you to be strategically (even boringly) consistent? Or do you need to renew your missional passion, to fall in love with your calling and minister again like all eternity hangs in the balance?

Once you have your one area, look to Jesus. He was unwaveringly confident in the one who sent him and would never leave him. He was consistent to the core, always and only about his Father's business. And he bled the mission. He bled it on the cross, shedding his innocent blood to cover our sins.

If your organization seems out of balance, remember, we reproduce what we are.

- Insecure leaders produce insecure followers.
- Unpredictable leaders produce hesitant followers.
- Self-centered leaders produce resentful followers.

With God's help, you are becoming a centered leader. You are filled with inner confidence in God's power within you. You are assured "that he who began a good work in you will carry it on to completion until the day of Christ Jesus" (Phil. 1:6). Because you are filled with the same Spirit who raised Christ from the dead, you are strategically consistent. You understand that successful leaders do consistently what others do occasionally. And you are mission focused. You are consumed by your why, and that drives your what. Because of who Jesus is and because of what he has done, you are part of the greatest mission on earth. You are not just building a church. You are filling heaven.

It Factors

- *It* is always a work of God. God does it through people, and God can choose anyone he wants to.
- You can position yourself to be a stronger candidate for God to choose.
- Leaders who have *it* don't just motivate, they inspire.
- There are many ways to inspire, but the most effective is to provide centered leadership. Centered leadership is secure, confident, fully engaged, guided by values, and obsessed with the mission.
- Uncentered leaders create unsettled followers.
- Off-center leaders are annoyingly insecure and produce insecure followers.
- Off-center leaders are consistently unpredictable and produce hesitant followers.

- Off-center leaders are distastefully self-absorbed and produce resentful followers.
- Centered leaders have an inward confidence in God that is substantial and enduring.
- Centered leaders are strategically consistent—relentless and boring. They find out what works and do it over and over again.
- Centered leaders are mission driven. They are consumed by the mission and keep it front and center for their organization.

Questions for Discussion or Reflection

1. Do you find yourself motivating your team (you feel like you are pushing people to do what they don't want to do) or inspiring them (pulling out the best from people's hearts)?
2. If your team understood centered and uncentered leadership, do you think they would describe your leadership as more centered or uncentered?
3. Be honest: Which is the biggest struggle in your leadership—being annoyingly insecure, consistently unpredictable, or distastefully self-absorbed?
4. Whichever is your greatest area of needed growth, what are you going to do about it? Who could help you?

CHAPTER 14

Do You Have *It?* Does *It* Have You?

> *One of the qualities of liberty is that, as long as it is*
> *being striven after, it goes on expanding. Therefore,*
> *the man who stands in the midst of the struggle and*
> *says, "I have it," merely shows by doing so that he*
> *has just lost it.*
>
> **—Henrik Ibsen**

In this chapter, I'm going to be honest about something I rarely share.

When I came to Christ, I had *it*. When I went into ministry, I lost it. I'll tell you the whole story, but I really don't want to. It's just so painful. But I am going to share it because I pray it helps you and because it's the most important issue we'll cover in this entire book.

If you want your ministry to have *it, you* must have it.

If you want your ministry to have *it, you* must have it.

When *it* has filtered through your heart—that rare combination of passion, integrity, focus, faith, expectation, drive, hunger, and God's anointing—God tends to infuse your ministry with *it*. He blesses your work. People are changed. Leaders

215

grow. Resources flow. The ministry seems to take on a life of its own. At times it seems like you're just hanging on for your life.

Have you noticed that new believers often have *it*? They're "unreasonably" excited about Christ. They think God is always speaking to them (and it's likely he often is). They see everything as spiritual (and they're probably right). They believe Jesus might return soon (and he very well could). Everything they do is focused on him.

They have *it*.

Then some "more mature" believer decides to help them grow up. "This is just a phase you're going through," the mature believer explains. "It's exciting, but it will wear off." The seasoned person might describe how Moses once experienced God's presence and glowed. But the glow faded.

What happens? The reasonable, longtime, passionless Christian inadvertently talks the new passionate believer into surrendering *it* and becoming like the rest of the dull Christians.

Something similar occasionally happens to ministers. Well-intentioned believers gladly surrender their lives to full-time vocational ministry. They dream of devoting the balance of their days to glorifying God and serving his people. Over time, though, the purity of their motives becomes clouded. They "turn pro." Without realizing it, they position themselves for promotion, posture to be noticed, or play church politics. They might market themselves "in the name of Jesus." They "build their brand" (whatever that means). They get their name "out there." Over time, they change. What was once beautiful turns ugly.

How I Lost *It*

So here's the part where I'm going to be painfully honest. I pray it helps you.

When I came to Christ, I had *it*. I knew God was with me. I knew God was speaking to me. I knew God was guiding me. God seemed to bless whatever I touched.

At the age of twenty-three, as a brand-new pastor, I had far more passion than wisdom. Like many wonderfully young and naive pastors, I didn't know what couldn't be done. If I believed God led me to do something, even if everyone else disagreed, I followed what I understood to be God's voice.

At the time, I was acutely aware of what I didn't know. Without a seminary degree, I felt only slightly better than biblically illiterate. (I had learned that Job is pronounced jobe and not job. That's an embarrassing mistake I won't ever make again.) With limited leadership experience, I relied more on prayer than knowledge. Without great leadership experience, I simply tried to treat people with love. Without tons of resources, I trusted God to use what little we had.

As a young pastor, with little thought about my future, I was simply trying to follow Jesus. Then one day someone told me I might actually become a good pastor. I'd thought of God as a good God, but never of myself as a good minister. Those words rattled me, scared me, haunted me. Could I really become a good pastor? Maybe so. But if I could become a good pastor, then the opposite was also a possibility. I could be a *bad* pastor.

How could I ever become good enough? If I became good enough, could I stay good enough? What if I was good one day and not the next? I was emotionally thrust back to the brief time I spent in sales. My old boss used to tell me I was only as good as my last sale. I was beginning to feel the same way in ministry. I was only as good as my last sermon. Or the last meeting. Or the last membership class. Or my last hospital visit. I felt a pressure I'd never known before.

Without realizing it, I took my focus off God's power and put it on my performance. Almost instantly, I felt like I didn't have as much time to read and enjoy God's Word. Instead, I had to produce challenging and engaging messages with catchy titles, memorable illustrations, and emotional endings. Sermon preparation became a cheap substitute for real time in God's Word. Instead of praying passionately and consistently, my longest prayers were now usually the ones I prayed in public. Instead of developing friendships with people who didn't know Christ, I worked hard to appear spiritual in front of those who already did.

After years of having *it,* I unknowingly abandoned it and tried to produce my version of it in my own strength.

It didn't work.

Shifting from *It*

No one would have noticed outwardly what had started to happen inwardly. My focus had shifted—ever so slightly. I wasn't consumed by bad things; I just wasn't consumed by the best things. I was more concerned with issues that had never before crossed my mind. I became obsessed with numbers, all sorts of numbers. Instead of measuring success by my obedience to God, I measured success by how many people showed up and how many guests returned.

I was also driven by appearances. With all my heart, I wanted to be that good pastor. Since people offered more verbal feedback than God did, they became my primary audience. I wanted them to know how hard I worked, how much I cared, and how devoted I was.

It's difficult to describe, but while doing the work of God, I wandered away from God. So many of us do. As pastors, we whole-heartedly believe that God exists, but we often do ministry as if he doesn't. Our sermons are filled with faith, but too often our actions prove we are devoid of it. Our public prayers declare that all things are possible with God, but our leadership style says all things are possible *if* we work hard enough.

John the Baptist said in John 3:30, "[Jesus] must increase, but I must decrease" (NKJV). In ministry, sometimes we try to increase by our own efforts, not realizing that we're dialing down the influence of Christ. You could say as we increase, *it* decreases.

Looking for *It* in All the Wrong Places

In the early years of our church, even though we had very few resources, we had God's presence and blessing. That's all we really needed. We had *it* in our hearts. That passion for him, mixed with his Spirit, won people to Christ. As our church grew, so did our resources. (Remember, *it* is not a result of resources—buildings, signs, mailings, lights, videos—but it does attract resources.) Suddenly we could buy things that earlier were barely even a dream.

We could buy children's curricula. We could start a Mother's Day Out program. We could print four-color bulletins. We could buy each staff member a computer. We could afford a video projector. (We could even find a volunteer with all ten fingers to run it!) We could buy stage lights that didn't explode. If we didn't have something, we could just purchase it.

Don't miss the subtlety of what happened. When we had limited resources, we thought God was all we needed, and he was the answer to all our problems. Then, as we had increasing resources, we thought we needed them, and they became the answer to all our problems. Without realizing it, our team started to think, *If we don't have* it, *we can work for it, buy it, or create it.* Along the way, we lost our focus on the one it was all about.

In the beginning, God was it. He was everything we needed. Now we thought we needed certain things to grow. It became less about God and more about everything else. And as you might expect, we started to lose *it*. Why? Because when you trust in the physical instead of the spiritual, you'll always lose it.

What happened? It was as if our *it* tank sprang a slow, small leak. Over time, *it* wasn't as special as it was before. Not as many people came to Christ. Fewer gave sacrificially. The amount of people willing to serve decreased. The number of those who simply consumed increased. It became clear that we were losing *it*. We decided we had to get it back.

When you trust in the physical instead of the spiritual, you'll always lose *it*.

Unfortunately, in our minds that meant more creativity, more hard work, more ministries to draw more people. We were wrong. We had slipped into the dangerous belief that we could create *it*, or recreate it. In a subtle (but sick) way, it stopped being about God and became about us.

Looking back, it seems so obvious. Back when we had *it*, we had vision alignment and divine focus. Now with all the resources, we had the option to do new things. Just because we could didn't mean we should, but that didn't stop us. We tackled new projects right and left while slowly walking away from what made *it* special in the first place.

In the early years, we had unmistakable camaraderie. We were a team. But as we wrongly came to believe we needed *things* to produce *it*, we started to vie for resources. Instead of completing each other, we competed with each other. Team members became more self-centered, territorial, and dangerously competitive.

Earlier, with nothing much to lose, we regularly took big risks. Year after year, we boldly declared, "We are faith-filled, big-thinking, bet-the-farm risk-takers. We will never insult God with small thinking and safe living." But that was easy to say when we were just getting started. Now that we had something to lose, we became more cautious, guarding what we already had. Instead of saying, "What do we have to lose? Let's go for it!" we found ourselves saying, "We have so much at stake. We'd better play it safe." Instead of leading with faith, we started living in fear.

It's amazing how ugly an it-less ministry can become. Whereas we were once generous and kingdom minded, we now had an unhealthy preoccupation with any church that was doing well. *What's their secret? How can we compete? Why is God blessing them more than he is blessing us?* Slowly but surely, we were killing *it*.

One of the bigger blows to *it* was hiring new staff and recruiting volunteers without communicating what *it* was all about. We assumed they would understand the heart of it. In the old days, everyone did. But as new members joined the team, they misinterpreted it. Many simply didn't get it. What made the ministry special before were the unseen qualities in people's hearts. The new staff members didn't know the story, so they thought what made *it* special was what they *could* see: the lights, the videos, the fancy kids' rooms. To have *it*, they assumed, we needed more bells and whistles. But what we really needed was more of what we had left behind: raw passion for God and for people.

Do You Have *It*?

In 1986, I graduated from Ardmore High School. (And you didn't send a graduation present. I'm still waiting.) That same year, *Top Gun* became a summer blockbuster. (Which was the graduation present I really needed, because a few people thought I looked like a not-quite-as-attractive Tom Cruise.) If you are old enough, you may remember the classic bar scene where Maverick and Goose sing "You've Lost That Lovin' Feeling" to Charlie (played by Kelly McGillis). In the summer of 1986, I loved that song. Even today, the words are hard to forget. *You've lost that lovin' feeling.*

Are you singing a similar lament right now? Do you need to humbly admit, "I've lost *it*"? Losing it is always painful.

You wouldn't be the first to lose ground. You can see people lose it in virtually every segment of society. A country can be a world power for decades or centuries before quietly fading. Companies rise and fall. Ministries climb and crash. Stocks soar and dip. A sports team may dominate one year and be at the bottom of the pack the next. Someone has a TikTok clip go viral. They're hot. Then days later, they're not. Actors and actresses are "in" one month and "out" the next. Same with politicians, pastors, plumbers, pediatricians, professors, painters, podcasters, and pig farmers. Just because you have *it* doesn't mean you're guaranteed to keep it.

Do you have *it*? Not did you use to have it. Do you have it today? Present tense?

Be honest. Do you have that something special that is only from God and only for God? Do you think more about pleasing him than strategizing how to grow your church? Do you desire his pleasure more than the applause of the crowd? Are you more concerned with his opinion of you than with the opinions of people?

Hopefully you can confidently answer those questions with God-honoring responses. If so, you probably have *it*.

For years, I couldn't. I wanted to be noticed, appreciated, affirmed, admired. I needed people to think well of me, speak highly of me, admire my leadership success. Sure, I wanted to see people get saved and grow spiritually, but if I was honest, that wasn't what was driving me. Instead, I was haunted by the desire to prove myself to some unknown something or someone. If I did more, accomplished more, reached more, had more followers, then maybe I'd be good enough.

If that's you today, you might do what I did. Cry. Repent. Plead with God, *God, give it back! Please! Give it back to me in a way that I'll never lose it again.*

Getting *It* Back

How do you get *it* back?

If I could put *it* in a bottle and give some to everyone, I'd do it in a second. But God is the one who gives it. And he seems to give it to those who want it—or to be precise, to those who want him more than anything else. Maybe it's time for him to become the true center of your life and then for you to ask him for *it*.

I'll share with you my journey with God and how I got *it* back. Hopefully my story will spark your desire to pursue God again with your whole heart.

How did I get *it* back? First, I had to admit I had lost it. That was hard for me. It probably won't be easy for you. By nature, most ministry leaders want to believe they're right and they're succeeding. Admitting failure—especially spiritual failure—is tough. (My failure was a spiritual one.) You might start with the confession, "I've lost *it*. I've taken my eyes off the prize. I've been distracted from a wholehearted pursuit of Christ."

Is it possible you have gotten slightly, or more than slightly, off track? Maybe you:

- Allowed some sin into your life.
- Neglected some basic spiritual disciplines.
- Read your positive press and started believing it.
- Became sick of the criticism and got ticked off.
- Saw your social media presence grow, and didn't notice your pride growing right along with it.
- Gave and gave and gave and forgot how to receive from others.
- Were hurt by someone close to you and, as a result, walled up.
- Offered your best, but it didn't feel like your best was good enough.
- Simply got tired and let down your guard.

Whatever the situation, if you had *it* and lost it, admit it. That's what I did.

Second, decide to get *it* back. You have to want it. Joe Ballard said, "It makes you more hungry after losing it last year." If you've lost it, maybe you'll now be hungrier for it than ever before. But let me be honest: some small adjustment isn't likely to bring it back. If all you needed was to tweak something, you'd have done that long ago. I'm guessing it'll take a significant change of direction or priorities. If you think you've found a quick fix, I guarantee that's not an it fix.

In my case, I had to force myself to do something I considered pretty radical. I was so caught up in the ministry world that I was neglecting my relationship with God. It's safe to say I was obsessed with ministry. I read church magazines. I listened to pastors' sermons. I watched certain Christian broadcasts. I read my favorite pastors' books. I attended the best church conferences. I devoured podcasts. I did these things and more—all the time.

Church consumed me. Church was first. God was second. Okay, it was worse than that. God was fourth or fifth.

My role as a pastor was interfering with my passion for God, which ricocheted back and crippled my role as a pastor. It was time to finally do something about it. Since I couldn't quit the ministry to redevelop my love for God, I simply quit devouring distracting ministry information. I felt God wanted me to tear down my ministry idols. This was right for me. The same approach might not be the right thing for you. But you may find this idea sparking another equally weird but divinely necessary one in your heart.

For two years, I fasted from ministry information. No more ministry books, ministry magazines, church conferences, other pastors' sermons. Extreme, I know. Instead, I read the Bible. And I prayed. And I fasted. And I read the Bible some more. Slowly, I started to fall in love with God again—not with his bride, the church. (She already has a husband, and it's not me.) The Holy Spirit was doing something special in my heart and the intensity increased each day. It was like I was being born again, again. By that, I'm not making a theological statement; I'm just describing my perception of the experience. I did not lose my salvation only to regain it. I had lost that loving feeling but found *it* again in a new and meaningful way, and I pray I'll never lose it again.

The apostle Paul started a well-known church in Ephesus. In many ways, this church had *it*. Years later, John, who helped oversee this church after Paul, recorded a message from Jesus to the Ephesian church in Revelation 2:4–5. Jesus said, "Yet I hold this against you: You have forsaken your first love. Remember the height from which you have fallen! Repent and do the things you did at first" (NIV 1984).

Have you forsaken your first love? Be honest. Do you love ministry more than you love Christ? Do you care more about what people think about you than what God thinks about you? Do you strategize ways to grow your ministry more than you think about how to grow God's people? Do you study the Bible to preach more often than you study it to hear from God? Do you pray more often in public than you do in private?

Have you lost your first love?

Jesus said to remember the height **Have you lost your first love?** from which you've fallen. Can you think back to a time when the only thing that mattered was what mattered to God? Do you remember craving his Word? Do you remember being excited about sharing your faith with anyone who would listen? Think back on what you had with God, that something special which may now be gone.

Jesus said, "Repent," or in other words, "Turn around." Stop doing what you've been doing. Do what you used to do. If you used to pray, pray. If you used to fast, fast. If you used to love freely, love freely. If you once gave until you had little left and then you gave some more, give that way again. If you used to worship while driving, without caring who saw you, start worshiping again. If you used to have intimate spiritual friendships but got too busy, rekindle those relationships or start new ones. If you used to serve people with no strings attached, start serving again.

Several months ago, I had lunch with a pastor friend. With deep emotion, he explained to me how he'd lost it. One of his board members left the church and took several key church members with him. This pastor's church was behind budget. He didn't want to preach. He didn't want to visit anyone in the hospital. He didn't want to read God's Word. He didn't even want to pray. After unloading plenty of hurt, my friend confided in me that if he weren't the pastor of his church, he wouldn't worship there.

I listened quietly, asking God for wisdom. I recognized his pain, understood his frustration, and related to his spiritual burnout. Knowing he needed my prayers more than my limited advice, I just asked him if we could pray. Without much enthusiasm, he agreed to let me. I simply asked God to "disturb him" in a big way.

Nothing significant happened that day.

A couple of months later, my friend called and shouted, "I'm disturbed! I'm disturbed!" He explained with great joy how God had disturbed him. My friend had suddenly become disgusted with his sin of spiritual complacency. He was disturbed by the lukewarmness in his church. He was disturbed by those in need. He was disturbed by people who were without Christ.

As he opened God's Word, his hunger for God increased. Deciding to fast, he denied his body nutrition, seeking only to be filled by God. With time, his compassion for people grew, his passion to preach increased, and he fell in love with Jesus again—all by doing the things he did at first. God disturbed him, in the best sort of way.

It happened to him, and it can happen (again) to you.

One Sunday, I preached on 2 Kings 6, telling the story of when a young man lost a borrowed ax head in a body of water. Panicked, the man cried out to the prophet Elisha. With faith from heaven, Elisha tossed a stick into the water where the heavy ax had sunk and God miraculously floated the ax to the top of the water. The key theme of the sermon? *God will help you find what you didn't mean to lose.*

That afternoon, Amy and I sat on our sofa reflecting on that idea. She started to cry, telling me she would give anything if God would help her find her wedding ring, which she had lost nine months earlier. When it happened, we had all searched the house up and down hoping to find her lost treasure, but to no avail. Finally, we had given up hope and quit.

But those words from the sermon seemed to renew our faith. *God will help you find what you didn't mean to lose.*

God (and Amy) as my witness(es), at that moment I felt strangely and unusually prompted. I walked straight across the room to a chair, lifted the back cushion, reached deep into the piece of furniture, and pulled out her missing wedding ring.

We cried. We laughed. We worshiped. We praised God.

I would find it hard to believe that story if I didn't live it myself. Whether you care about the ring or not, I hope you care about the truth.

God will help you find what you didn't mean to lose.

If you've lost *it,* God knows where it is. He will help you find it and get it back. You find it by doing the things that once brought it to you. Your relationship with God is only as good as you want it to be. You will get what you put into it.

So what are you waiting for? *It* is waiting, and it is time to seek him. Now.

It Factors

- If you want your ministry to have *it,* more important than anything else we've discussed, *you* must have it.

- As we increase, *it* decreases.
- God is what you need and is the answer to your problems.
- If you think you can buy *it,* you've already lost it.
- You might need to start with the confession, "I've lost *it.* I've taken my eyes off the prize. I've been distracted from a wholehearted pursuit of Christ."
- Ask God to give *it* back.
- To get *it* back, do the things that brought it before.
- God will help you find what you didn't mean to lose.

Questions for Discussion or Reflection

1. Name someone or some organization that had *it* and lost it. What do you think happened? Why did they lose it? What do you think it would take for them to get it back?
2. Do you have *it?* If so, what is contributing to it? If the answer is no, when did you start to lose it? What changed in you? How have you taken your eyes off Christ?
3. How well are you communicating the heart of *it* to those who are new to your ministry? Do new attenders get it? What about volunteers? How about staff members? If they don't understand what God is doing, how can you better express it?
4. If you've lost *it,* it will probably take more than some small adjustment to recover it. What radical step could you take to get it back (or to get more of it)? What about the leaders of your church? Is there something you used to do that contributed to *it* that you no longer do? What is God calling you to do that you have been neglecting?

Conclusion

How to Keep *It* Once You Have It

*I consider my life worth nothing to me; my only aim is
to finish the race and complete the task the Lord Jesus
has given me—the task of testifying to the good news of
God's grace.*

—The apostle Paul (Acts 20:24)

I am sitting at my computer with tears forming. I am praying,
but not with words. This prayer is born in my heart. At this
moment, I am so aware of God's presence. He is here with me. It's
4:23 a.m., and I'm sitting at the kitchen table, typing these words,
overwhelmed by God. As I'm typing—or trying to—I am worshiping him, needing him, crying to him. Nothing is wrong. My family
is healthy. Our church is growing. Life is good. Yet everything is
wrong. As good as everything appears, I'm in spiritual agony. I
hurt for people, deeply. I cry often. I wake up at night and pray for
hours before falling back to sleep. I'm consumed by the burdens
of God. Others see our church and say it is succeeding. I feel like
we're failing.

We're so big. We've done so little.

It's not that I'm depressed. It's quite the opposite. The fire of God's presence is burning within me, consuming me. When I say "consuming me," that's exactly what I mean. It is burning away the worst parts of me. I can relate to Paul's words: "I have been crucified with Christ and I no longer live, but Christ lives in me. The life I now live in the body, I live by faith in the Son of God, who loved me and gave himself for me" (Gal. 2:20).

I have *it*—again.

And I never want to lose it.

We've come a long way together on our journey. We've seen how it-full ministries have a God-inspired vision and are focused on the things that really matter. We've embraced the truth that with-it people share *it* in a deep and sincere camaraderie. Our ministry innovation has increased because of our increasing passion to share the gospel. We've acknowledged that we won't succeed at everything and that failing is often a step toward succeeding. We're excited that as God gives us hearts that are focused outward and are kingdom minded, he tends to give us more of *it*. Most of all, we've recognized that for our churches to have *it*, *we* need to have it.

If you don't have *it*, I pray you'll get it back. Once you get it—the passion, the fire, the purity, the hunger for God—I pray you'll keep it always. I know what it's like to have it and lose it.

I want to always walk closely with God, enjoying his consistent presence and direction. So I've made three prayers a part of my daily prayer life. These heartfelt and dangerous prayers have helped me to keep *it*.

Stretch Me

When you become comfortable and complacent in your relationship with God, you'll lose *it*. Comfort is the enemy of faith. Complacency is the poison that pollutes passion. Hebrews 11:6 says, "And without faith it is impossible to please God." Jesus pleaded with his followers, knowing the time was short, reminding them always to "be on guard! Be alert!" (Mark 13:33). That's why we want to ask God constantly to stretch us.

Years ago, while swimming with my kids, I met another dad who was an executive coach. After some casual conversation, he asked me in a competitive dad-to-dad sort of way, "How long do you think you can hold your breath underwater?" Even as a middle-aged dude, I could feel the rush of excitement as I anticipated a contest between men. *He doesn't know who he's talking to,* I thought smugly. *I grew up watching Aquaman!*

"I don't know," I replied, my heart pumping. "Maybe a minute." This was quite a humble response; I secretly believed I could do more than that.

He challenged me to give it a try, and seconds later I was underwater ready to prove my Aquamanhood.

As the seconds slowly ticked by, I felt my lungs tighten. Panic set in. *Can I drown doing this?* Deciding that drowning is better than losing, I stayed under. I could feel my face turn blue. My eyes opened wider. *Longer. Longer. Just a few seconds longer.* Finally, after what seemed like a lifetime, I burst out of the water gasping for air. I was still alive!

The coach smiled and said, "Impressive! You stayed under for one minute and twelve seconds!"

That's what I'm talkin' about.

The coach said, "What would you say if I told you that I could help you double your time?" *What?* I'd been played. He wasn't going to compete against me. *Wimp!* He was trying to teach me some sort of I'm-a-coach-and-you're-not lesson. Maybe he didn't know that I'd just almost died.

"You're smoking crack," I blurted. "That's what I'd say."

The coach continued, in a prepare-for-Yoda-to-teach-you-the-power-of-the-Force-my-young-Jedi kind of way, "If you pay attention, I'll teach you something that will inspire you to do even more than you've ever done before."

He had my full attention.

The coach talked to me almost hypnotically, explaining a calming technique that was sure to increase my time. "You can do much more than you realize," he assured me. "Your body can survive underwater for several minutes. Your greatest limitation is your mind. You must silence your mind. Your body can do more than your mind can understand. Take four deep breaths. Inhale as much oxygen as you can. When you do, you are expanding the capacity of your lungs. Slide slowly into the water. Close your eyes. Remain perfectly still. When your lungs tighten, don't worry. You still have a lot more time. When you think you can't go on, open your eyes. Focus on something. Count slowly to twenty. When you get to twenty, count again."

Armed with this advice, I followed his instructions. After four breaths, I calmly slid underwater. I tried my best to turn off my mind. When my lungs tightened, I relaxed. When I hit my limit, I opened my eyes and counted. Then I counted some more. Every few seconds, my coach said, "More . . . you have more in you. More . . . you have more in you."

Finally, I had enough and came up for air. This time when I came out of the water, my coach was beaming as he told me that my new record was 2:45. Do you understand those numbers? There was a two and a forty-five and that two-dot thingy in the middle. Two minutes and forty-five seconds!

I was elated, pumped, jazzed, and shocked. *How did I do that? I stayed underwater for almost three whole minutes.* I didn't know I had that in me.

Then the coach looked me in the eye and said, "You have more in you than you realize. God has put more in you than anyone knows."

God spoke to me that day. It was about more than oxygenation potential. That's why I now regularly say to him, *Stretch me.*

I'd like to say that coach's words to you. You have more in you than you realize. God has put more in you than anyone knows.

Ask God to stretch you. He wants to. He wants you to live by faith, to believe him. It will mean putting yourself in new environments, experiencing something different.

> You have more in you than you realize. God has put more in you than anyone knows.

Ask God to stretch you, then follow his direction. He might direct you to change your leadership style or the way you preach. He might challenge you to go to a developing country and leave behind part of your heart. He might ask you to give like you've never given before. He might lead you to do something your closest friends believe is foolish and impossible. He might introduce you to a new church leader who will rock your comfortable world, or maybe to a lost person who desperately needs God.

Let him stretch you. Attempt what others say can't be done. You have more in you than you realize. God has put more in you than anyone else sees.

Ask God to stretch you. As he does, you might start to find *it* again.

Ruin Me

On Sunday, October 8, 1871, Dwight L. Moody was finishing his Sunday evening sermon when the city fire bell began to ring. Realizing that much of the city was burning, Moody's first concern was for his family. Rushing to close his sermon, he asked the people to evaluate their standing with God and return the next week. Little did he know, many of them would never return. They died in the worst fire in Chicago's history.

Later, Moody agonized, wondering whether any of the deceased had died without Christ. They were in his church building and he let them leave without confronting their sin. Broken and changed, Moody vowed to God he'd never hold back again. Every time he stood before a crowd, he pled with them to follow Christ. D. L. Moody was ruined—in a very good way.

Whenever I meet someone who has *it*—a heart abandoned to Jesus—I'm meeting a ruined person. I'm not talking about a destructive ruin. Sin destroys and ruins. Burnout can destroy and ruin. Anger can destroy and ruin. No, I'm referring to the work of a loving God who breaks us and ruins us for his glory. Josh Billings said, "Life is short, but it's long enough to ruin any man who wants to be ruined." Maybe it's time to let God ruin you.

Let me explain. I told you about the coach who helped me learn to hold my breath. That short drill in the pool started what became a strong friendship. The friend I made that day in the pool is named Mark Button. Mark has *it*. He was the cofounder of Koosh Toys, developers of the Koosh ball and the vortex football. (I invented a technique that allows me to throw a vortex football farther than you ever could. Seriously, I'm ready when you are. Bring it on.) (My Koosh ball skills are not so impressive, but give me time.)

It took time to hear all of Mark's story. When he unfolded it for me, my appreciation for him quickly grew into a profound love and deep respect. For several years, Mark and his wife, Ronnie, tried to get pregnant. They were disappointed month after month. After years of shattered expectations, Mark and Ronnie discovered they were pregnant. Not with one child, not with two, but with triplets! God had answered their prayers. Times three.

Or so they thought.

The pregnancy progressed perfectly until Mother's Day. That was the day Ronnie was admitted to the hospital with an excruciating headache and died suddenly, along with her three babies, the victim of a brain aneurysm. I have to wipe tears away every time I think about Mark's loss. He had sold his company. They had purchased their dream home. They had finally become pregnant, with triplets. Mark had everything a person could want but lost the people he loved the most.

Ruined.

This tragedy happened more than twenty years ago. Since then, Mark has remarried and God has blessed his new family with healthy children. When I asked him what he's most excited about today, he looked at me sincerely and said, "God uses me to ruin people." Because of his business experience, Mark has many influential friends. His goal is to take some of the greatest leaders in the country to one of the poorest corners of the world and ruin them.

Mark exposes people to things they prefer to ignore and lets God wreck them. Do you want *it?* Ask God to ruin you in a good way. Let him break your heart. Allow him to give you a divine discontent. Let God crush you with a burden.

As I look back on my life, when I had *it,* I was ruined. God had messed me up for his purposes. All I thought about was him. Pleasing him. Obeying him. Talking about him. When I saw people without Christ, my heart ached for them. Sharing Jesus consumed me. I wasn't good for much else. I was ruined.

Over time, though, I slipped back into normal routines. I didn't care as much about people. I didn't care as much about God. I wasn't ruined anymore, and I didn't have *it.*

Like Isaiah, I was of more use to God when I was ruined. You might relate to an incident in Isaiah's story recorded in Isaiah 6. (I wrote a whole chapter about Isaiah's experience with God in my book *Dangerous Prayers: Because Following Jesus Was Never Meant to Be Safe.*) It was the year King Uzziah died. Because King Uzziah had been such a godly and influential king, it felt like "the year the world as we knew it ended." In the worst time Isaiah could imagine, he saw the Lord. And he got *it*. Verse 5 records his thoughts when he experienced the pure presence of God: "Woe to me!" he cried. "I am *ruined!* For I am a man of unclean lips, and I live among a people of unclean lips, and my eyes have seen the King, the LORD Almighty" (emphasis mine).

Isaiah was never the same. He had experienced God. The encounter squashed him flat, squeezed out all his pride, and emptied him of self-ambition. Now he was suitable for God's purpose, for the greatest fulfillment Isaiah could ever find. With *it,* Isaiah was now fully available to God. When God asked who he should send with a message to his people, Isaiah blurted, "Here am I. Send me!" (v. 8).

As I reflect on the seasons of my life when I lived without *it,* I remember God trying to ruin me. But I fought it off. In ministry, I had built a wall of protection around my heart. Honestly, I thought it was a strength, something necessary to survive.

Whenever I visited with someone who was hurting, I separated my feelings from the conversation, thinking it would help me be a better pastor. When someone faced a tragedy, like an accidental death or a suicide, I managed to stay strong, never showing weakness.

Maybe you've fallen prey to the same fallacy. You might think, *But if I allow myself to break down, I'll be a wreck for my family. I won't be able to survive emotionally. The people who trust me will stop consulting me.* Yes, those are legitimate concerns, but you might be surprised by the actual results of dropping your emotional shields. Your family might be overjoyed to share with you in your hurts. God might sustain you emotionally and spiritually in ways that have never crossed your mind. Those who look to you could be inspired by your vulnerability. Sure, it will feel risky. But it's riskier to stay walled up.

Over the years, God exposed me time and again to things that could've ruined me in a good way. On April 19, 1995, Timothy McVeigh detonated a bomb across the street from the church I served in Oklahoma City. That bomb killed 168 people. The shock waves traveled across the globe as CNN showed pictures of the carnage. For me, it was more than images flickering on the TV screen. The rescue workers used our church lobby as a morgue. When I walked by and saw the mangled bodies of men, women, and little children, my stomach turned, but I didn't let it ruin me.

When I visited the poor in a developing nation and held the tiny fragile hands of children who hadn't eaten for days, it bothered me, confused me, shook me. Seeing these innocent children suffering aroused a mix of emotions—rage, depression, and everything in between. Although this experience could have ruined me in a good way, I somehow managed to stuff the emotions and get back to life as normal.

God tried to ruin me. I didn't let *it* happen.

My wife's brother, David, died at the age of thirty-four. To say this impacted a lot of lives would be the understatement of this book. Seeing our family let him go was the thing that somehow startled me back to my neglected spiritual reality. His funeral was one of the more sobering moments of our lives. Life is short. Eternity is real. I wasn't doing much about it.

That's when I started to evaluate my leadership at the church. From an outsider's perspective, we were wildly successful. But were we really? Would it really matter in our communities if our church wasn't there? Were my motives pure? Was God pleased? Was I being obedient as a leader?

Finally, I surrendered. Completely. Totally. Fully. Holding nothing back. With a repentant and soft heart, I wanted *it* back—the zeal for him, the desire to please him, the passion for people. So I said from the deepest place in my heart, *Okay, God, you want to ruin me, go ahead. Do it. Ruin me through and through.*

He did.

Now instead of being rock solid in my emotions, I cry often. I tear up when people hurt. I carry their burdens home with me. I care deeply about people who are in need. Suffering bothers me. Injustice haunts me. When someone I know is hurting, it wrecks me.

> If you want to keep *it*, and I know you do, ask God to ruin you.

If you want to keep *it*, and I know you do, ask God to ruin you. Expose yourself to something that you know will move you. Don't shrink back. Don't fight your emotions. Don't lay another brick atop your self-made wall of protection. Give in to the heart. Feed the hurt. Let *it* grow. Let it bother you. Invite it to overtake you.

God loves to give *it* to ruined people.

Heal Me

I pray God is stretching you. I pray he will ruin you. My third prayer is that he will heal you. And he will, if you sincerely ask him to. You might think, *But I'm not sick.* Maybe not physically, but if you're like most people I know, you have some wounds God wants to heal.

To be healed, we have to first admit the ways we're sick or in need. You might have to face something you've stuffed, ignored, or rationalized for years. Are you ready to confess your need? To make it easier on you, I'll go first.

I'm an addict.

No, I don't have a sexual addiction. I'm not addicted to alcohol, illegal drugs, prescription medicine, or the lottery. And I'm not going to deliver a clever punch line like, "Actually, I have three addictions—to the Father, Son, and Holy Spirit!" or, "I'm addicted to studying the Bible." I have a serious addiction that I'm working hard to overcome.

Truth is, many of us are addicted. Some addictions are frowned upon. Others often go unmentioned. Some are even readily accepted. You might have one of the "acceptable" addictions. For example, some are addicted to:

- pleasing people
- perfection
- social media
- working out
- work

Me? I'm addicted to adrenaline. You could say I'm an adrenaline junkie.

You might think, *Well, that's no big deal.* Actually, it *is* a big deal. It's dangerous. I'm fighting to overcome it. My body craves the adrenaline rush. Usually adrenaline is a good friend. God gave our bodies adrenaline to handle challenging situations. But for some of us, our bodies crave the rush of that performance-enhancing hormone.

Here is how it affects me: If there are no leadership emergencies, I subconsciously crave some problem to solve. I desire action. When things are slow, I panic and create things to do. I have a hard time relaxing. And I mean a *very* hard time. When I do relax, it usually means doing a high-intensity workout, playing competitive tennis, or listening to a book related to work, ministry, or leadership.

In other words, I don't often relax.

Way too many times, I'm with my family, but I'm not all there. Like this week. Just yesterday, Amy and I visited our daughter Mandy and her husband, James. Mandy is in the early stages of her pregnancy. As the three of them brainstormed baby names, I sat in their house, in the same room, with my laptop, working on this book. Sick. I know. I had been doing better recently. But I've slipped back into some bad and dangerous patterns.

In the evenings when my teenagers are nearby (only home for a short time before launching into adulthood), my mind is often consumed by church-related thoughts. I'll never forget the heartwrenching moment almost two decades ago when my third daughter, Anna, with tears in her eyes, asked, "Why don't you listen to me when I'm talking? Do you even love me?" Sobering words. That's why I'm working hard. I've *got* to change. And I do. I'm better for a while. For weeks and even months, I keep things in perspective. When I'm with family, I'm fully present. When I'm off work, I'm really off. Then occasionally I slip back. Like a recovering alcoholic might "fall off the wagon" into a dangerous binge, I fall back into work storms and find it almost impossible to stop.

On a good day, I'm alive, engaged, full of joy, and fully available to those I love. On a bad day, when my family begs for my attention, my mind is generally racing, working, strategizing. When I do finally relax, generally after about four days off, my body starts to thaw out. I can feel my heart rate and breathing slow. My face tingles. Once I finally settle down, I become nice, laid-back Craig—until I go back to work and the dangerous cycle repeats itself.

Can you relate? Maybe it's not an addiction to adrenaline, but you might have an equally dangerous and vulnerable need. To be honest, I've been talking with a counselor for help. For years, I thought seeking professional help was a sign of weakness. I couldn't have been more wrong. Together, with the help of my wife, my counselor, and my close friends, I'm working to make progress. Before some recent steps backward, I had been doing so much better. Obviously, I still have more work to do.

Will you be honest with yourself for a moment? Do you have a hard time trusting? Have you been burned by church members and find it difficult to have friends? Are you distant from your spouse? Do people tell you that you're a control freak? Do you find yourself on a high when people brag on you and a low when they criticize you? Do you feel good about yourself when your ministry is growing and depressed when it is not? Do you constantly compare yourself with others on social media, and hate it when you do? Do you have a secret sin? Or a fantasy life? Are you overly critical and jealous? Are you jealous when other pastors succeed? Do you feel like you never quite measure up? Call out to God, your ultimate healer.

I've shared with you three prayers that are an important part of my life. I'm wondering, should they have a place in your life?

Stretch me.

Ruin me.

Heal me.

May God Bless You

Thank you for hanging in there with me through this whole book. We've traveled a long way together. It has been an honor to share with you. Parts of the book may have been painful to read. Parts were certainly painful for me to write. Hopefully God is stirring you, drawing you, speaking to you. When he does, I know you'll follow his lead.

Before wrapping up, I'd like to encourage you to spend time with the leaders of your ministry. Discuss the questions at the end of each chapter. You might have *it,* but those you're with might not. I believe God wants to use you to help them get it.

Once you do get *it,* never take it for granted. Embrace the power of the Holy Spirit working in you to do more than you can ask or imagine. To help you get it and keep it, I'll share part of a Franciscan benediction. This is my final prayer for you:

May God bless you with discomfort at easy answers, half-truths, and superficial relationships, so that you may live deep within your heart.

May God bless you with anger at injustice, oppression, and the exploitation of people, so that you may work for justice, freedom, and peace.

May God bless you with tears to shed for those who suffer from pain, rejection, and starvation, so that you may reach out your hand to comfort them and to turn their pain into joy.

And may God bless you with enough foolishness to believe that you can make a difference in this world, so that you can do what others claim cannot be done.

That's *it*. Amen.

It Factors

- When you become comfortable and complacent in your relationship with God, you'll lose *it*. Comfort is the enemy of faith. Without faith, it's impossible to please God.
- Your greatest limitation is often your mind. Your body can do more than your mind can understand.
- Let God stretch you. Attempt what others say can't be done. You have more in you than you realize. God has put more in you than anyone else sees. Ask God to stretch you. As he does, you might start to find *it* again.
- If you want to keep *it*, ask God to ruin you. Expose yourself to something you know will move you. Feed the hurt. Let it grow. Let it bother you. Invite it to overtake you. God loves to give *it* to ruined people.
- To be healed, we have to first admit the ways we're sick or in need. You might have to face something you've stuffed, ignored, or rationalized for years. Are you ready to confess your need?

- Once you do get *it*, never take it for granted. Embrace the power of the Holy Spirit working in you to do more than you can ask or imagine.

Questions for Discussion or Reflection

1. How are you allowing God to stretch you in your church leadership? What do you need to expose yourself to in order to break out of a slump? Is God leading you to attempt something that you've not yet attempted? What are you going to do about it?
2. What is God using to ruin you in a good way? Is there something that bothers you that you've been avoiding?
3. Do you have an addiction you need to address? Does a part of your heart need healing? Have you been hurt or disillusioned and need God's healing? What do you think God wants to do about it?
4. Reread the Franciscan benediction. What is God saying to you through that prayer? What is God saying to the leaders of your ministry?

Acknowledgments

To all of my friends who helped make this message possible, I'm ridiculously grateful for you.

My wife, Amy Groeschel: I've loved you with all my heart for more than three decades, and I love you more today than ever before. How's that even possible? You are my dream girl.

Vince Antonucci: What a ride! You are a gift to me both as a friend and a partner in the work of the kingdom. Thank you for your love and passion for this message. It shows and means more to me than I can express. You unquestionably have *it* (and we might even say you are full of it). Working with you is one of the greatest honors of my ministry and leadership. Let's keep working together until we die or until Jesus comes back.

Katherine Fedor: You have the spiritual gift of "perfection." Thank you for sharing your gift with our church family and for your contribution to this book.

Webster Younce, Andy Rogers, Brian Phipps, Curt Diepenhorst, Paul Fisher, and the rest of the team at Zondervan: It's truly an honor to do another book together.

Mark Schoenwald and Don Jacobson: You promised to raise the standard, and you kept your word. Thank you for leading like *it* matters.

Tom Winters: Are you tired of me yet? How many books have

we done together? Fourteen? Fifteen? Thank you for being a feisty agent, a faithful part of our church family, and a trusted friend.

Adrianne Manning: You are the best at what you do. My life, my family, and our ministry are better because God sent you. You can never leave. If you try, we'll just go with you.

To you, the reader: Thank you for caring about God's bride, the church. What you do is important. Your leadership strengthens churches, empowers people, changes lives, and impacts eternity. Leadership will always be hard. Don't get discouraged. You are never alone. Whatever you do, lead like *it* matters.

Notes

1. Thom S. Rainer and Eric Geiger, *Simple Church* (Nashville: B & H Publishing Group, 2006), 76.
2. Stephanie Armour, "Friendship and Work: A Good or Bad Partnership?" *USA Today,* August 1, 2007, www.usatoday.com/money/workplace/2007 -08-01-work-friends_N.htm.
3. "American Individualism Shines Through in People's Self-Image," Barna Group, July 23, 2007, www.barna.com/research/american -individualism-shines-through-in-peoples-self-image/.
4. "First Hot Air Balloon," Bible.org, July 15, 1993, www.bible.org /illustration/first-hot-balloon.
5. Kathy Sierra, "Sometimes the Magic Is in the Imperfections," *Creating Passionate Users* (blog), December 19, 2006, headrush.typepad.com /creating_passionate_users/2006/12/sometimes_the_m.html.
6. Tom Kelley, *The Ten Faces of Innovation* (New York: Currency, 2005), 2.
7. Seth Godin, *Small Is the New Big* (New York: Penguin, 2006), 124.
8. Christian Smith with Melinda Lundquist Denton, *Soul Searching: The Religious and Spiritual Lives of American Teenagers* (New York: Oxford University Press, 2005).
9. Evie Liu, "McDonald's and Other Fast Food Chains Should Keep an Eye on Chick-Fil-A," *Barron's,* June 10, 2019, www.barrons.com/articles /mcdonalds-has-a-real-competitor-in-chick-fil-a-51560162600.
10. Mark Horwitch and Meredith Whipple Callahan, "How Leaders Inspire: Cracking the Code," Bain & Company, June 9, 2016, www.bain.com /insights/how-leaders-inspire-cracking-the-code/.
11. Quoted in Adam Bryant, "In Head-Hunting, Big Data May Not Be Such a Big Deal," *New York Times,* June 19, 2013, www.nytimes.com/2013/06/20 /business/in-head-hunting-big-data-may-not-be-such-a-big-deal.html.

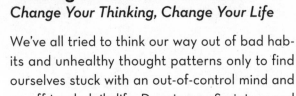

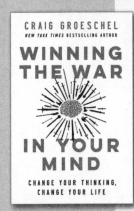

Winning the War in Your Mind
Change Your Thinking, Change Your Life

We've all tried to think our way out of bad habits and unhealthy thought patterns only to find ourselves stuck with an out-of-control mind and an off-track daily life. Drawing on Scripture and the latest findings of brain science, Pastor Craig Groeschel lays out practical strategies that will free you from the grip of harmful, destructive thinking and enable you to live the life of joy and peace that God intends for you. It's time to change your mind so God can change your life.

Dangerous Prayers
Because Following Jesus Was Never Meant to Be Safe

Do you ever wonder, "Why doesn't God answer my prayers?" Pastor Craig Groeschel will show you how to pray the prayers that search your soul, break your habits, and send you to pursue the calling God has for you. Discover the power of authentically communicating with God, breaking out of the restrictive "spiritual safety bubble," and expanding your faith in what is possible with God, gaining the courage it takes to pray dangerous prayers.

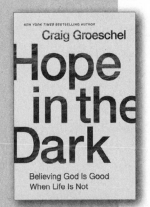

Hope in the Dark
Believing God Is Good When Life Is Not

In the midst of great pain, we may wonder whether God really cares about us. Pastor Craig Groeschel invites us to wrestle with our questions and doubts while honoring our faith and asking God to heal our unbelief. Rediscover faith in the character, power, and presence of God.

The Christian Atheist
Believing in God but Living As If He Doesn't Exist

Join Pastor Craig Groeschel for a frank and raw conversation as he unpacks his personal walk toward an authentic, God-honoring life.

Liking Jesus
Intimacy and Contentment in a Selfie-Centered World

Learn how breaking unmanageable digital dependencies can bring a balance of spiritual depth and human engagement back to your life.

Soul Detox
Clean Living in a Contaminated World

Examine the spiritual toxins poisoning your relationship with God and learn about ways to remain focused on God's holy standards.

Fight
Winning the Battles That Matter Most

Uncover your true identity as a powerful man with a warrior's heart and find the strength to fight battles you know must be won.

Divine Direction
Seven Decisions That Will Change Your Life

Take your life to wonderful and unexpected places only God could have planned by understanding how the choices you make connect you to God.

Daily Power
365 Days of Fuel for Your Soul

Develop a consistent, daily pursuit of Jesus as Pastor Craig Groeschel shares insights from his life that you can apply to almost every area of your own life.

YouVersion

Bring the Bible into your everyday life.

YouVersion creates experiences that encourage and challenge people to seek God every day.

Access hundreds of Bible versions, reading plans, prayer guides, podcasts, and more.

Find practical leadership insights,
discover more books from Craig, and
see where Craig will be speaking next.

craiggroeschel.com